DOWN THE RABBIT HOLE An OSINT Journey

Open Source Intelligence Gathering for Penetration Testing

Chris Kubecka

Down the Rabbit Hole: An OSINT Journey Open Source Intelligence Gathering

Published by Chris Kubecka & HypaSec

HypaSec is a registered entity in the Netherlands Commercial Registration: 63945517

Printed in the Netherlands
First Printing
ISBN: 978-0-9956875-4-7

Publisher: HypaSec, Netherlands
Graphics: Chris Kubecka
Technical Editor: P. Spencer
Indexer: Chris Kubecka

Library of Congress Cataloguing-in-Publication Data

Application Submitted

British Library Cataloguing-in-Publication Data

Application Submitted

Why down this rabbit hole?

The secret of freedom lies in educating people, whereas the secret of tyranny is in keeping them ignorant.

- Maximilien Robespierre

Initially, this book began as a presentation at the Cyber Senate Industrial Control Cybersecurity Nuclear Summit in Warrington, UK. Originally, I intended to use some of the same techniques to target a nuclear power plant or someone in a nuclear regulatory capacity. After submitting my original talk idea. Daesh, otherwise known as ISIS, began publicly threatening the European nuclear industry. I work with nuclear power plant and enrichment operators giving lectures on cyber awareness. Due to the threats, Belgium evacuated all non-essential personnel from nuclear facilities. I decided it was not in anyone's best interest to give a how to target nuclear installations and changed the target instead to the law firm behind the Panama Papers fiasco.

The project further expanded for another to include additional targets for the Cyber Senate Industrial Control Cybersecurity conference in Sacramento, USA, and OpenFest in Sofia, Bulgaria. I chose a mostly political slant. 2016 was a very tumultuous year in politics. Brexit, Trump, and the rise of the interesting politics and coups in Turkey, Netherlands, Germany, Russia, Bulgaria and the Philippines. It's a lot more fun to learn about a topic in an empowering way. Also, only politicians like politicians. They make a fun target.

Table of Contents

Why OSINT rocks!

Open source intelligence gathering (OSINT) and web-based reconnaissance is an important part of penetration testing and proactive defense. The more connected we are, the more information is held about everything. Yummy, juicy information for both a penetration tester or a malicious actor. Learning what sources of are available to start your search is an important first step in learning about reconnaissance and how the information could be utilized or resold. Both issues you or your client need to know. All of the tools and techniques in this book can be ninjafied with Python, Ruby or PowerShell.

Target Audience
Penetration testers, security and network analysis or anyone curious about open source intelligence gathering. Particularly those with a slight political slant.

Organization of the book
A slightly evil hacker perspective cookbook loaded with happy hacker fun time examples. The information provided is meant to inspire the reader towards their journey in OSINT.

Chapter 1: Why Open Source Intelligence gathering?
There are many ways to get to a target, but you must discover them first. That's where OSINT comes in, part of the reconnaissance phase of penetration testing

Chapter 2: Setting up your OSINT lab
Get your virtual machine and tools setup and prepared. If you already have FOCA, Maltego and Spiderfoot installed and configured with API keys.

Chapter 3: Targets
Learning should be fun. The example targets are a law firm, political

parties, politicians, and election boards.

Chapter 4: Netcraft
Utilizing the research and database from Netcraft. System uptime, we page technologies, banner grabbing and more information from a distance.

Chapter 5: Robtex
The NSA Swiss Army Knife of the internet. Discover the entire target known public network IP infrastructure and blacklist status.

Chapter 6: Search Engine/ Google Dorking
Search engines are your friend: they want to help you find juicy files and vulnerable systems.

Chapter 7: WikiLeaks.org & Other Leaky Databases
Leveraging previous leaks about your target from leaky databases. A social engineer's wet dream.

Chapter 8: Censys & Shodan
Alternative search engines that index asset services not web page indexing. Revealing vulnerable systems through banner grabbed services.

Chapter 9: Spiderfoot
Retrieving information from multiple sources for OSINT with Spiderfoot.

Chapter 10: Nmap/ZenMap
This multi-purpose tool is also useful for OSINT in addition to general scanning.

Chapter 11: FOCA
Document metadata information collection. Usernames, network information, and other useful tidbits.

Chapter 12: Maltego
Transforming targets into information with APIs and a graphical interface.

Chapter 13: Vulnerabilities & Exploitation
Research target vulnerability information and potential exploits.

Companion Website

The companion website for the book is at, at **https://hypasec.com/tools.** Here you will find downloads, URL links, tips and tricks and any errata.

Chapter 1

Falling in love with OSINT

INFORMATION IN THIS CHAPTER:

- What makes OSINT relevant to penetration testing
- Where real attackers spend their time
- OSINT and Social Engineering with OSINT
- Case Study: Shamoon 2

CONTENTS

Give me six hours to chop down a tree and I will spend the first four sharpening the axe.

- Abraham Lincoln

1 Why Open Source Intelligence Gathering?

This book is a hands-on learning journey. It's written from a hacker perspective, not a law enforcement perspective. There is a huge difference. This book won't teach you the fine art of skip tracing or finding a person for bounty. It will help to reveal IT vulnerabilities which can be sold or exploited. Along with other pieces of information helpful for a penetration test. These basic techniques can be ninjafied with Python and scripting. Broken down into recipes with easy to follow step-by-step instructions to enable your OSINT journey.

As you read this book. Imagine for a moment. You are paid to work from anywhere in the world with a good internet connection to be part of a penetration testing team. Your role is to be part of the reconnaissance phase, step one during the test. Your primary goal is to find out as much as possible, as quickly as possible. Everything and anything relevant you can discover remotely. The goal is to get the information, not to break or exploit systems.

In real life, attackers can spend anywhere from 80%-90% of their time in the reconnaissance part of their attack; penetration testing is not that much different. Perhaps the client wants to know mainly IT, IoT or ICS vulnerabilities. Some will want to know much more about their public exposure and internet exposed assets. If an organization is proactive in its defense, OINT is crucial.

Benefits of OSINT

- OSINT is powerful
- OSINT is low cost and can be high return on investment
- Open source tools are available
- Can be performed remotely
- Requires an internet connection
- OSINT is fun, as long as you're not the target

If you've ever watched a USA based gangster, mobster or a bank robber movie. Prior to actually robbing the bank, stealing the jewels, etc. It's carefully planned out. They "scope" the joint, slang for reconnaissance. The ultimate goal is to get the goods and get out without getting caught. To avoid jail; reconnaissance is a crucial step to accomplishing the final plan and not getting caught.

A target can be "sized" up, profiled. By performing reconnaissance, a tester or adversary can find obvious weaknesses, employee usage, sensitive documents, ways in or information to use against a target to gain entry. Defensive and offensive technology, personnel and services can also be profiled. A classic method of getting into organizations is social engineering via phishing. It starts with reconnaissance and OSINT. Even the biggest companies, like Saudi Aramco, have almost fallen because of phishing and adversarial usage of OSINT.

What information makes good OSINT? Time relevant + accurate data + target relevant = actionable OSINT.

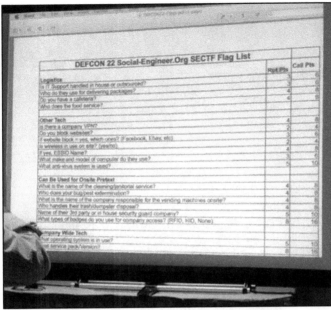

Figure 1 Defcon 22 Social Engineering contest goals

A summary of what OSINT some social engineers look. A picture I took a at Defcon 22, the largest hacker convention in the world. A capture the flag contest, for social engineering.

Information	Points
Is IT outsourced or in-house?	10
Who's the target's delivery company?	6
Does the target have a canteen?	8
Is there a VPN?	8
What are the blocked or allowed websites?	10
What make and model of computers are in use?	6
What anti-virus does the target use?	10
What operating system is used by the target?	10
What operating system service pack/version is in use?	10
Any Wi-Fi in use?	4
Which websites are blocked?	6
Who does the food service?	8
What is the Wi-Fi SSID name?	8

In 2012, Saudi Aramco suffered a near catastrophic cyber-attack, leading to a loss of about 85% of their Windows based systems. Saudi Aramco is the world's most valuable company. They are worth trillions, producing around 25% of the world's energy from their oil, petrochemical and joint ventures. This attack was called Shamoon, named from a snippet of the malicious code. The attackers used social engineering, spear-phishing, weak IT security and a time bomb to execute. The logic bomb was timed during a low staffing period, Ramadan. On August 15th, 2012 the master boot record of hard drives began being wiped, along with massive amounts of data and logs.

Was it Iran? Was it hacktivists named Cutting Sword of Justice? Attribution is a major challenge when dealing with an attack. Especially one that damages logs and evidence.

Fast forward to 2016 & 2017. Saudi Aramco and other Saudi government and related organizations took precautions against Shamoon 1 by implementing virtual desktops (VDI). Using the VDI technology minimized risk of wiping the master boot record by recording and loading virtual desktops instead of the using a local hard drive. Using social engineering, phishing, Word document macros. Sadly, Huawei, the VDI vendor, had hard-coded credentials listed in user manuals. Attackers advanced Shamoon into version 2. This new version aimed to take out the VDI infrastructure put in place to avoid some of the primary risks associated with Shamoon 1.

In both cases, attackers used OSINT to profile the targets. Also, always read the manual, they contain gems of information.

References

Bisson, D. (2017, 1 12). *Second Wave of Shamoon 2: Disttrack Can Now Wipe Organizations' VDI Snapshots*. Retrieved from The State

of Security: https://www.tripwire.com/state-of-
security/security-data-protection/cyber-security/second-
wave-shamoon-2-disttrack-can-now-wipe-organizations-vdi-
snapshots/

Kubecka, C. (n.d.). DefCon 22 Social Engineering CTF. *DefCon 22 Social Engineering CTF*. HypaSec, Las Vegas.

Paganini, P. (2017, January 10). *A Second variant of Shamoon 2 targets virtualization products* . Retrieved from Security Affairs: http://securityaffairs.co/wordpress/55235/malware/shamoon-2-virtualizations.html

Pagliery, J. (2015, August 5). *The inside story of the biggest hack in history.* Retrieved from CNN Tech: http://money.cnn.com/2015/08/05/technology/aramco-hack/index.html

Wikipedia. (2017, May 17). *Wikipedia.* Retrieved from Saudi Aramco Cyber Attack. https://en.wikipedia.org/wiki/Saudi_Aramco#Cyber_Attack

Chapter 2

Getting your tools ready

<table>
<tr><td>

INFORMATION IN THIS CHAPTER:

- OSINT Kali distribution information & setup
- Setting up Windows tools
- Installing OSINT tools on a Kali distribution
- Obtaining API keys
- Installing and configuring Spiderfoot
- Installing and configuring Maltego
- Tool download URLs

</td><td>

CONTENTS

</td></tr>
</table>

It's best to have your tools with you. If you don't, you're apt to find something you didn't expect and get discouraged.

- Steven King

2 How to Setup your OSINT Lab

There are some essential tools required to setup your OSINT lab. They aren't too complicated and shouldn't cost any additional money. Some of the tools do have commercial versions. If you download anything, check the hash MD5 + SHA-1 or SHA-2 256 or above. MD5 is too short, so should not be relied on solely. Also, check files with anti-virus or Virustotal.com. Be safe when setting up your lab. Another way to keep safe, using virtualization and sandboxes. If you are introducing your testing machine into a client environment, don't infect the customer.

Penetration testing machines are only that, for penetration testing. Out of the box, Kali isn't configured for security. They are setup to test other machines, not to be tested. There are modules in Kali tools that can attack other Kali machines. Keep that in mind when setting up and securing your lab. Don't check your online banking, get sensitive data off, harden where possible.

Lab requirements

- ☑ A good, fast, relatively uncensored internet connection.
- ☑ A computer with at least 2GB extra RAM to dedicate to Kali and other tools
- ☑ If you use Kali, a computer that can run it with some basic Linux knowledge
- ☑ You may need to install additional tools
    - ○ VM Player or Workstation Pro version 12 & above
    - ○ Spiderfoot
    - ○ VM Ware Fusion
    - ○ Open Box virtualization
    - ○ Kali Linux 64 bit based image
- ☑ A Shodan.io account and API Key
- ☑ API Keys and accounts for Spiderfoot, described in detail in the Spiderfoot setup section
- ☑ API Keys and accounts for Maltego, described in detail in the Maltego setup section
- ☑ FOCA Pro

Using the OSINT Kali Distribution, a custom distribution. Is by far, the easiest way to setup your lab. It already has Spiderfoot installed; as well as, all the regular 300+ installed Kali tools.

If you want or need to setup your lab from scratch. Offensive Security, the company behind Kali have many different types of Kali images. You can run in a Live configuration, ARM, VM, Hyper-V, Raspberry Pi, etc. Most images available for download will work as long as Spiderfoot can be installed. Kali comes with Nmap and Maltego Community Edition (CE) but requires Spiderfoot for some of the exercises.

If you don't want to use Linux at all. The tools and labs can be run on a Windows based machine, version 7 or higher. You would need to install Spiderfoot, Maltego Nmap and FOCA Pro. FOCA only runs on Windows.

OSINT Kali Distribution Information

The book OSINT Kali distribution is available from the companion website: **https://www.hypasec.com/Tools.html** or the listed Torrent. It is built on the standard 2017.1 version of Kali from Offensive Security but updated and customized. The book distribution has the following features:

- The network on Ethernet, which is eth0 is DHCP. You can change this if required for your network. This can change depending on your configuration.
- Firefox web browser
- Nmap 7.50
- Metasploit 4.14.27-dev
- Maltego 4.0.11.9357-0kali1
- OWASP ZAP 2.60
- Spiderfoot 2.90
- GUFW 17.04.1-1 which is a graphical firewall, easier than IP Tables
- VMWare 12 compatible
- 2GB RAM, 1 Processor
- 60 GB hard drive
- Network is Bridged

OSINT Kali64 in WM Player/Workstation/Fusion 12

Using the book OSINT Kali distribution is the easiest way to begin. This version is for version 12 of VM Ware. It uses the proprietary format of VM Ware.

Open VMWare Player, Fusion or Workstation 12. It will bring up a welcome page. On the welcome page, chose **Open a Virtual Machine**. Browse to the folder where you the extracted image. Open the **Clone of OSINTKali64.vmx** fil. VM Ware will import the virtual machine. Press the **Play virtual machine** button. The Kali machine will open. When prompted, enter the username and password to log in as root.

Username: **root**   Password: **Lamarr**

OSINT Kali64 OVF in VM Player/Workstation 12

OVF is an exportable format with OpenBox and VMWare compatibility. There are some caveats: OVF can act oddly sometimes for no known reason after conversion. To be on the safe side, make copies, snapshots, and backup as required.

Open VMWare Player, Fusion or Workstation 12. It will bring up a welcome page. On the welcome page, chose **Open a Virtual Machine**. Browse to the folder where you the extracted image. A Pop-up box will appear, Keep or change the name, then pick a Storage path for the new virtual machine. Click the **Import** button.

You will probably get another pop-up warning/error which tells you: The import failed because it didn't meet the hardware specification… Press the **Retry** button. Your machine will import in a few minutes. Press the **Play virtual machine** button

Username: **root**   Password: **Lamarr**

Setting up FOCA Pro on Windows

1. Download FOCA Pro at **https://www.elevenpaths.com/labstools/foca/index.html**
2. Extract to a folder of your choice
3. Open the FOCA folder
4. Run the FOCAPro.exe to install and start.

Setting up Spiderfoot on Windows

1. Download Spiderfoot at **http://www.spiderfoot.net/download/**
1. Unzip
2. Install in a folder of your choice
3. Run the EXE to install and start

Setting up Maltego on Windows

1. Download Maltego at **https://www.paterva.com/web7/downloads.php**
2. Unzip
3. Install in a folder of your choice
4. Run the EXE to install and start

Install OSINT tools on a Kali Linux 2017.1

Installing the tools on Kali is easy. Download the Kali image which fits your needs at the Offensive Security website **https://www.offensive-security.com/kali-linux-vmware-virtualbox-image-download/**. Install following the Offensive

Security directions. Next, install the OSINT tools.

Tool	Type in bold as root # to install/upgrade
Upgrading Maltego CE	# apt-get update && apt-get install maltegoce
Upgrade NMap/ZenMap	# apt-get install nmap
Installing GUFW	# apt-get install gufw
Update Metasploit	# service postgresql start # msfconsole msf> msfupdate msf> exit # msfconsole
Installing Spiderfoot	# cd/opt # ls You should see a directory called "Teeth" # git clone https://github.com/smicallef/spiderfoot ./spiderfoot # cd spiderfoot # pip install lxml netaddr M2Crypto cherrypy mako You might get a warning pip install upgrade is ready # pip install --upgrade # python sf.py Spiderfoot will start in the terminal. To access Spiderfoot go to http://127.0.0.1:5001

Email Account Helper Tool 10-Minute Email

Before creating new accounts and registering. Since this is a lab environment, use more anonymous, temporary email account. There are many websites which offer this free service. You get a temporary email account good for 10 minutes or more to register for API keys and vendor accounts. Most of the temporary email providers are not secure, so don't use the temporary email account for anything personal or vital.

Figure 2 10-Minute temporary email account

10-Minute email or other variants. They come in many languages. There is 20-minute email, 30-minute, etc. Put 10-minute email in a search engine and utilize to setup your lab accounts.

Obtaining API Keys

To search databases effectively on the internet, you need API keys. You will need to setup some accounts to get API keys, using 10-minute email or similar.

Botscout API Key

1. Go to **http://www.botscout.com/getkey.htm**
2. Create an account and log in
3. Under Account Info, your API key will be there

Cymon.io API Key

1. Go to **https://cymon.io**
2. Signup for Cymon
3. Fill in username, email and password
4. Request API key

Project Honeypot API Key

1. Go to http://www.projecthoneypot.org
2. Sign up and log in
3. Click **Services** -> **HTTP Blacklist**
4. An API key should be listed

Malware Patrol Receipt ID

1. Go to **http://www.malwarepatrol.net**
2. Create an account and log in
3. Click **Open Source** and scroll down to the bottom
4. Click the **Free** link in the subscription pricing table
5. Click the **free block lists** link
6. You will receive a receipt ID

Shodan API Key

1. Go to **http://www.shodan.io**
2. Sign up and log in
3. Click **Developer Center**
4. On the far right your API key should appear in a box

Passive Total API Key

1. Go to **https://www.passivetotal.org/registration**
2. Sign-up and log-in
3. Go to **Settings**
4. Go to **API Access**
5. Click **Show** and it will show your Key and Secret

VirusTotal.com API Key

1. Go to **http://www.virustotal.com**
2. Sign up and log in
3. Click your username in the far right and select **My API Key**

XForce API Key

1. Go to **https://exchange.xforce.ibmcloud.com/new**
2. Create an IBM ID and log in
3. Go to your account settings
4. Got to **https://exchange.xforce.ibmcloud.com/**
5. Click your **Profile**
6. Click **Settings**
7. Click **API Access**
8. Generate the API key and password (you need both)
9. More information :
   https://api.xforce.ibmcloud.com/doc/

Clearbit

1. Go to **https://dashboard.clearbit.com/login**
2. Create an account and sign in
3. Click the API link on the left side of your account screen

AlienVault OTX

1. Go to **https://otx.alienvault.com/**
2. Create an account and sign in
3. In your account settings towards the bottom of the page is the OTX Key value

Hunter.io

1. Go to **http://www.hunter.io**
2. Create and account and sign in
3. Click API to view the API Key

Configuring Spiderfoot and API Keys

Spiderfoot scans can take hours. Configuring it with API keys will lower the rate of false positives. Saving time and effort. There is minor configuring.

1. Start Spiderfoot by the EXE in Windows
2. Terminal in OSINT Kali:
   a. **# cd/opt/Spiderfoot**
   b. **# ./sf.py**
3. In a browser open **http://127.0.0.1:5001**
4. Chose **Settings**
5. Chose **Global Settings**
6. Add in Google's public DNS server of **8.8.8.8**. You can change this to your needs, including internal DNS servers.

Global Settings

Option	Value
Enable debugging?	False
Override the default resolver with another DNS server. For example, 8.8.8.8 is Google's open DNS server.	8.8.8.8

Figure 3 Spiderfoot Global Settings

7. Chose **Historic**
8. Change the default Wayback machine days and add 180,300

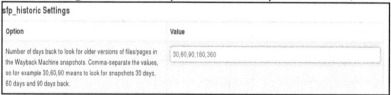

stp_historic Settings

Option	Value
Number of days back to look for older versions of files/pages in the Wayback Machine snapshots. Comma-separate the values, so for example 30,60,90 means to look for snapshots 30 days, 60 days and 90 days back.	30,60,90,180,360

Figure 4 Spiderfoot Historic Settings

9. Choose **Interesting Files**
10. Change the search engine, if you want from Yahoo to **Google**

sfp_intfiles Settings	
Option	Value
File extensions of files you consider interesting.	doc,docx,ppt,pptx,pdf,xls,xlsx,zip,jpeg,jpg,list,one,mdb
Number of search engine results pages to iterate through if using one.	20
If using a search engine, which one? google, yahoo or bing.	google
Use search engines to quickly find files. If false, only spidering will be used.	True

Figure 5 Spiderfoot interesting file extensions settings

11. Choose **BotScout**
12. Copy and paste the BotScout API key into the Settings -> BotScout section in Spiderfoot

sfp_botscout Settings	
Option	Value
botscout.com API key. Without this you will be limited to 50 look-ups per day.	

Figure 6 Spiderfoot Botscout settings

13. Chose **Cymon.io**
14. Copy and paste the Cymon.io API key into the Settings -> Cymon.io section in Spiderfoot
15. Chose **Honeypot Checker**
16. Copy and paste the ProjectHoneypot.org API key into the Settings -> Honeypot Checker section in Spiderfoot
17. Chose **MalwarePatrol**
18. Copy and paste the MalwarePatrol Receipt ID into the Settings -> MalwarePatrol section in Spiderfoot
19. Chose **Shodan**
20. Copy and paste the Shodan.io API key into the Settings -> Shodan section in Spiderfoot
21. Chose **VirusTotal**
22. Copy and paste the VirusTotal API key into the Settings -> VirusTotal section in Spiderfoot
23. Chose **XForce**
24. Copy and paste the XForce API key into the Settings -> XForce section in Spiderfoot
25. **Chose Clearbit**
26. Copy and paste the Clearbit API key into the Settings -> Clearbit section in Spiderfoot
27. Chose **AlienVault OTX**
28. Copy and paste the OTX key into the Settings -> AlienVault OTX section in Spiderfoot
29. Chose **Hunter.io**
30. Copy and paste the Hunter.io API key into the Settings ->

Hunter.io section in Spiderfoot
31. Press the "**Save Changes**" button at the top of the Settings page.

Configuring Maltego and API Keys

Setting up Maltego for Windows, OSINT Kali and Kali is the same. Register for a Maltego account at: **https://www.paterva.com/web7/community/community.php**

1. Get your Passive Total, VirusTotal and Shodan API Keys ready
2. Open Maltego
3. Register for an account or sign-in
4. You will enable all but one transform:

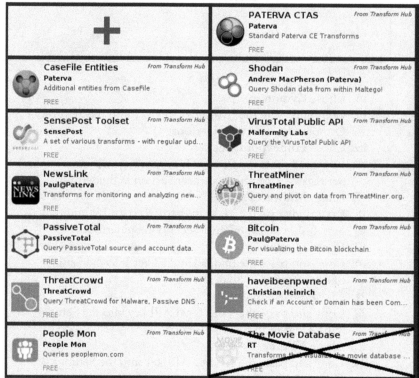

Figure 7 Maltego Transform options

5. For all the transforms but The Movie Database. Hover over the transform, click **Install**, **Yes**, then **Finish**.
6. For the **Passive Total, VirusTotal and Shodan** transforms. Hover over, click the Settings button, then enter the API keys, then click close.

Figure 8 Maltego Transform seed settings

Now you are all setup. Sit back, relax, have a glass of something you like to drink and feel good. Your OSINT environment setup is finished! Happy hacker face☺

References

Spiderfoot API Key documentation
http://www.spiderfoot.net/documentation/#api

URLs for tools:

Name	URL Location
OSINT-Kali Distribution	https://www.hypasec.com/Tools.html
Official Kali	https://www.offensive-security.com/kali-linux-vmware-virtualbox-image-download/
Spiderfoot	http://www.spiderfoot.net/download/
Maltego	https://www.paterva.com/web7/downloads.php
NMap	https://nmap.org/download.html#windows
FOCA Pro	https://www.elevenpaths.com/labstools/foca/index.html

Who's in the bullseye

CONTENTS

The art of war teaches us to rely not on the likelihood of the enemy's not coming, but on our own readiness to receive him; not on the chance of his not attacking, but rather on the fact that we have made our position unassailable.

- Sun Tzu

3 Targets

Learning a new technique is easier when it's fun. As such, I chose targets and case studies which gave me a happy hacker smile. There were several targets selected for this project: The targets are post-breach or election oriented.

Mossack Fonseca

The first target chosen was Mossack Fonseca, a law firm. Based in warm, slightly corrupt Panama, which currently scores an 87/130 rank and scores 38/100 in corruption. Mossack Fonseca has worldwide offices and web servers at the time of writing hosted in the USA. The law firm earned notoriety after a massive leak known as The Panama Papers. More recently, the founders of the law firm were arrested and held without bail or bond in Panama in 2017.

Figure 9 Maybe some of that spam wasn't phishing?

Much more in-depth information about the Panama Papers, key players, clients and the nitty-gritty is on Wikipedia. The story is still unravelling in courts all over the world.

Figure 10 Super-Secret Squirrel Spy Stuff

Democratic National Party

The Democratic National Party is one of two major political parties in the United States. The organization was the subject of a compromise and an email leak. Consequently, WikiLeaks posted many emails on WikiLeaks; where there is a searchable database. Blames was pointed towards Russian spies for the 2016 email breach and subsequent leaks.

Trump

Trump, a man of Huge™ words, tiny hands and out to make America great again somehow with bad hair and leaving behind a trail of broken, bankrupt businesses. Donald J Trump ran for the USA presidency and won. It isn't a reality TV show; it is real! There have already been several USA politicians who were celebrities, television, movie stars, a wrestler. Looking at the unique and eclectic mix of presidents past; his election is not that abnormal. Only in America.

Figure 11 Making America's bad hair great again! ™

In September 2016, the State of New York, USA Trump Towers $50,000.00 for weak security leading to compromised customer details. Working through the labs will show you how secure some of the Trump websites and business assets are.

Figure 12 The Grand Old Party

Republican National Party

Now that Trump is President of the United States of America, he leads the GOP. We will look at the opposing party to the Democratic National Party. They are the Republican National Party, also known as the GOP and formally known as the RNC. To be fair and less biased after reviewing the DNC, I decided to include them.

Geert Wilders & the PVV

Figure 13 Geert Wilders after his meeting with Le Pen

Geert Wilders and the Partij Voor De Vrijheid PVV Political Party are the most right wing party in the Netherlands. Nowadays, it seems fashionable to have shall we say, unusual hair as a politician. Geert Wilders is no stranger to making strong statements by video, speeches and his signature overdyed bottle blonde hair. With nicknames, such as "Mozart" and "Captain Peroxide." His speeches and party have an anti-immigration, anti-eastern European and anti-Islamic tone.

A video the PVV party released in 2008 called "Fitna" created controversy around the globe. It featured handpicked Sutras from the Quan alongside graphic images and videos from violent Islamic terrorist events. Ending with the assumed tearing up of a Quran in the background. Supposedly, per Wilders, it was not a Quran but a phone book, which was ripped up. The fallout was vocal and at times violent. Protests in numerous countries, withdrawal of some trade deals, criminal investigations into Wilders and acts of violence and terrorism. Pakistan, after attempting to get YouTube to censor the video. They tried to block YouTube but instead re-routed the entire internet through Pakistan then crashed the internet a little. I wonder if Pakistani security services were able to suck up all the re-routed unencrypted internet traffic?.

Dutch Voting Software and Election Board

Figure 14 Massive fears of Russian vote tampering in Europe

Voting tabulation software in use for the Netherlands and Germany for the 2017 election. Called OSV. Also, the Kiesraad.nl, the election office and board for the Netherlands. In 2009, a few countries in Europe reviewed the risks of electronic machine voting. They didn't like what they saw and made it illegal. Sorry, Diebold. However, although e-voting machines are illegal in the countries of the Netherlands and Germany, software to tabulate the votes are legal. Thanks to a Dutch hacker, named Sijmen Ruwof using OSINT skills, found critical security issues. Due to his write up, the Dutch Parliament voted to hand count all votes for the 2017 election. They will not use the vulnerable tabulation software. We'll look at his work with a slightly different perspective.

United Kingdom Independent Party UKIP

Figure 15 UKIP Party and other promises from Brexit

Nigel Farage and the UK Independence Party (UKIP) Political Party are a UK based, Eurosceptic, anti-immigration and right wing. Nigel leads the UKIP party and works as an EU representative in Brussels. Much of the party's platform, especially leading up to Brexit were antiimmigration, including European immigrants to the UK. Some think Nigel and his merry party of UKIP are out of touch with regular UK folks. Maybe, with some of the inflated, out of touch figures the party touted before the Brexit vote. Hmm....

References

Bloomberg. 2016. *Editor's Picks*. 2016 September. http://www.chicagobusiness.com/article/20160923/NEWS 07/160929874/trump-hotels-to-pay-50-000-fine-over-data-breaches.

Make your own funny Panama Papers memes with Funny Memes http://funnymemes.co/panama-papers-funny-meme/

Ruwhof, Sijmen. 2017. *How to hack the upcoming Dutch Elections* . 2 February. https://sijmen.ruwhof.net/weblog/1166-how-to-hack-the-upcoming-dutch-elections .

Wikipedia. 2017. *Wikipedia*. 1 January. https://en.wikipedia.org/wiki/Campaigning_in_the_United_Kingdom_European_Union_membership_referendum,_201 6#Grassroots_Out.

Wikipedia. 2016. *Wikipedia*. 19 September.
https://en.wikipedia.org/wiki/Democratic_Party_(United_S tates).

Wikipedia. 2016. *Wikipedia*. 13 March.
https://en.wikipedia.org/wiki/Panama_Papers.

Wikipedia. 2017. *Republican Party (United States)*. 30 January.
https://en.wikipedia.org/wiki/Republican_Party_(United_St ates) .

Chapter 4

Banner grabbing fun

| INFORMATION IN THIS CHAPTER: | CONTENTS |

INFORMATION IN THIS CHAPTER:

- Why Netcraft is useful and how to use it
- Netcraft site review for mossfon.com
- Netcraft site review for PVV.nl
- Netcraft site review for GOP.com
- Netcraft site review for UKIP.org
- Netcraft site review for DNC.org

War is an art and as such is not susceptible of explanation by fixed formula.

- General George Patton Jr.

4 Netcraft

Netcraft has website discovery tools which can give us a good deal of preliminary information about a target. Based in the United Kingdom (formerly part of Europe). They provide both free and commercial services. Commercially, Netcraft is well known for security testing and anti-phishing. Additionally, they provide market share, web server, operating system information, some security testing information, and the state related to networks on the internet. We will focus on the site report, which checks for:

- ☑ Date first observed
- ☑ System information
- ☑ Last reboot
- ☑ Operating system fingerprint
- ☑ Security trust information
- ☑ Mail Sender Policy Framework
- ☑ Web trackers
- ☑ Website technology

Netcraft Mossfon.com Site Report

Use an internet browser to go to: **http://toolbar.netcraft.com/site_report**
Enter the URL: **Mossfon.com.** Netcraft shows us the IP address of 199.83.135.15, hosted in the USA, first seen July 1997, operating system, traffic statistics and more is offered in the site report.

Data Type	Data
Site	http://Mossfon.com
Netbock Owner	Incapsula Inc
IPv4 Address	199.83.135.15
Domain registrar	Networksolutions.com
Operating System	Linux
Web Server	Apache 2.2.15
First seen	July 1997
Hosted Country	USA
Email SPF security	Pass = mx SoftFail = all
Domain based Message Authentication, Reporting and Conformance DMARC	No record
JavaScript	Uses JavaScript

The results are returned quickly and can be quite detailed. I summarised what was pertinent from my perspective. The target has been running a web server for a while. It is likely junk or unintended files left about on servers, publicly accessible. The web server version running is an outdated, unsupported and insecure version of Apache. The email security is contradictory. Pass SPF designates the host is allowed to send while SoftFail SPF specifies the host is not allowed to send but is in transition. Email insecurity is a great way for an attacker to get in a target network. Phishing, sweet phishing.

Netcraft PVV.NL Site Report

Use an internet browser to go to: **http://toolbar.netcraft.com/site_report**
Enter the URL: **pvv.nl.** Netcraft shows what operating system and web server is in use by the target.

Data Type	Data
Site	http://pvv.nl
Netbock Owner	Unknown
IPv4 Address	195.20.9.130
IPv6	2001:67c:28fc:195:20:9:130:0
Domain registrar	Unknown
Operating System	Linux
Web Server	Apache
First seen	January 2009
Hosted Country	NL
Nameserver	ns.eatserver.nl
DNS Admin	root@eatserver.nl
Reverse DNS	pegasus.eatserver.nl
Hosting company	Extraa Internet Solutions
DNS Security Extensions	Enabled
Email SPF security	Pass = a Pass = mx Neutral = all
Domain based Message Authentication, Reporting and Conformance DMARC	No record
JavaScript	Uses JavaScript

Hosting History	Apache
	Apache 2.2.17, DAV/2, mod_ssl/2.2.17, OpenSSL/1.0.0d in 2014

The Netcraft report returned different results for the PVV and could not pinpoint the current web server version of Apache running. The web server has both IPv4 and IPv6 addresses. The DNS server shown, could potentially be used in a DDoS attack to deny services. However, not likely to succeed with any lasting effect. But other types of DNS attacks come to mind when I see DNS servers. I was a good hacker and didn't try a DNS zone transfer as that would be illegal in most countries. The web server likely still uses a version of OpenSSL. But which version? It's important to know since some versions are vulnerable to exploit code via simple Google searches. The DMARC settings are non-existent which is typical. The SPF settings allow email MXs to send mail, the IP address matches the record but with the neutral setting says nothing can be said about its validity.

Netcraft GOP.com Site Report

Use an internet browser to go to **http://toolbar.netcraft.com/site_report.** Enter the URL: **gop.com.** Review and document results

Data Type	Data
Site	http://gop.com
Netbock Owner	Fastly
IPv4 Address	151.101.1.127
IPv6	Not present
Domain registrar	Unknown
Operating System	Linux
Web Server	Varnish
First seen	January 2009
Hosted Country	USA
Nameserver	ns-748.awsdns-29.net
DNS Admin	awsdns-hostmaster@amazon.com
Reverse DNS	Unknown
Hosting company	Unknown

DNS Security Extensions	Unknown
Email SPF security	Qualifier Mechanism Argument + (Pass) ip4 148.163.153.140 + (Pass) ip4 38.70.0.128/26 + (Pass) ip4 69.56.56.0/26 + (Pass) ip4 208.73.5.112 + (Pass) ip4 64.203.97.224/27 + (Pass) ip4 64.203.98.0/26 + (Pass) ip4 64.203.105.0/24 + (Pass) ip4 192.96.206.40 + (Pass) ip4 64.203.96.133 + (Pass) include netatlantic.com + (Pass) include spf.mtasv.net + (Pass) include mail.zendesk.com - (Fail) all
Domain based Message Authentication, Reporting and Conformance DMARC	No record
JavaScript	Uses JavaScript
Hosting History	Varnish 151.101.1.127 Linux 151.101.129.127 Linux 151.101.193.127 Linux 151.101.1.127 unknown 151.101.1.127 Linux 151.101.129.127 Linux 151.101.65.127 Linux 151.101.193.127 Linux 151.101.1.127 Linux 151.101.65.127 Linux

The GOP Netcraft result via the SPF settings show all the IP addresses and domains allowed to send email for the GOP domain. That's a whole lot of IP addresses and domains. I would feel very uncomfortable as the email administrator if I were security minded. The DNS and some of the infrastructure is on Amazon AWS. The AWS infrastructure makes it difficult to attack with a traditional DDoS. However, I smile ear to ear with the increased usage of IoT bot DDoS attacks. There is something oddly satisfying about knowing I could use code to attack a web server with your home refrigerator or security camera. One of the many IP addresses listed in the GOP SPF settings shows a high probability of being an IoT Ethernet thermometer.

The sheer amount of IP addresses and domains the GOP trusts with parts of their communications to me is astounding. Happy attack hacker face ☺

Netcraft UKIP.org Site Report

Go to: **http://toolbar.netcraft.com/site_report.** Enter the URL: **UKIP.org.** View the site report for **UKIP.org.**

Data Type	Data
Site	http://www.ukip.org
Netbock Owner	Akamai Technologies
IPv4 Address	92.123.72.177
IPv6	Not present
Domain registrar	Pir.org
Operating System	Linux
Web Server	Apache
First seen	May 2000
Hosted Country	EU
Nameserver	whois.123-reg.co.uk
DNS Admin	hostmaster@ukip.org
Reverse DNS	a92-123-72-177.deploy.akamaitechnologies.com
Hosting company	Akamai
DNS Security Extensions	Unknown
Email SPF security	None
Domain based Message Authentication, Reporting and Conformance	No record

DMARC	
JavaScript	Uses JavaScript
Hosting	Apache/2.4.7 Ubuntu
History	92.123.143.42
	92.123.143.88
	23.55.58.218
	23.55.58.186
	23.55.58.218
	23.55.58.186
	23.55.58.218
	23.55.58.186
	23.55.58.218
	23.62.3.128

The UKIP Netcraft results show zero effort at any email security via SPF. They too have had a long history of running a web server. Thoughts of dorking or juicy files come to mind. The version of the web server, Apache 2.4.7 is behind security updates. Yummy.

Netcraft DNC.org Site Report

Go to: **http://toolbar.netcraft.com/site_report.** Enter the URL: **DNC.org.** View the site report for **DNC.org.**

Data Type	Data
Site	http://dnc.org
Netbock Owner	Amazon.com, Inc.
IPv4 Address	54.192.28.161
Domain registrar	Pir.org
Operating System	Cisco
Web Server	Apache
First seen	Apr 2010
Hosted Country	USA
Nameserver	ns-1238.awsdns-26.org
DNS Admin	awsdns-hostmaster@amazon.com
Reverse DNS	server-54-192-28-161.dub2.r.cloudfront.net
Hosting company	Amazon
Email SPF security	+ (Pass) ip4 208.69.4.0/22
	+ (Pass) ip4 205.201.128.0/20
	+ (Pass) ip4 198.2.128.0/18
	+ (Pass) include amazonses.com

	+ (Pass) include sendgrid.net + (Pass) include servers.mcsv.net + (Pass) include spf.protection.outlook.com ~ (SoftFail) all
Domain based Message Authentication, Reporting and Conformance DMARC	p=none Requested handling policy None: no specific action to be taken regarding delivery of messages. pct=100 Sampling rate 100% of messages from the Domain Owner's mail stream should have DMARC applied. rua=mailto:dmarc@dnc.org Reporting URI(s) for aggregate data dmarc@dnc.org
JavaScript	Uses JavaScript
Hosting History	208.69.4.141 Cisco, DNC Webserver, Apache 208.69.4.10 F5 BIG-IP

The DNC Netcraft scan returns a bevvy of IP addresses and domains allowed to handle part or all of the DNC's email accommodations. Not as many as the GOP, but still makes me feel uncomfortable. The listing of an Outlook domain tells me instantly they use Microsoft Office, likely newest versions, with web-based access to email allowed. The DNC has also had a web server for a while. Anytime I see a web server or web page hosted for a few years. I usually find some juicy, not meant to be public stuff left up. Either by mistake, it was okay back then, well-meaning developers, administrator backdoors in many cases forgotten.

The DNC has the most explicitly restricted email from the Netcraft results but could give false assurances. None of the targets had great anti-phishing SPF settings. A shame considering some post breach after phishing attacks. The affected targets didn't perform good lessons learnt as part of the incident response plan. All of the targets are high value with a matching budget that can easily afford to hire the best political donations and offshore money can buy.

Back in 201X, I lead an incident investigation for an embassy email breach. The embassy, located in Europe was in a tight spot. The business email account suffered a compromised. Someone was sending extortion emails to other embassies from the hacked embassy business email account. To make matters worse, the attackers signed the emails with the name of the Ambassador's Secretary and said the money was for ISIS. To throw in more chaos to the mayhem mix. The embassy IT administrator had been on the job for less than a week with no handover from the previous person. The previous IT admin had no clue about IT security with 123456 as the password. It was one of those times in my life I wondered what the f*ck I did for a living and questioned my sanity.

The embassy mistrusted the Diplomatic Police due to politics, and local law enforcement had no jurisdiction. Embassies are very political places; not everyone is friends. All sorts of mystery, intrigue and uncomfortable yet important meetings are held in these mini-seats of power. Due to citizenship, previous experience in similar matters and dumb luck I took on the role. Compromising a high-value email account gave the attackers access to contacts and high-value communications. It was beyond ugly.

Prior to the current beheading, truck driving, suicide bomber tw*t image, they are known for now. Daesh made millions from various companies and many countries via kidnap, ransom and extortion. Initially, the attackers asked for 25K Euro from a handful of countries. The Diplomatic Police proactively sent out an alert to all the embassy business email addresses in the To field, not BCC. The attackers still had access to the communications via an email forwarder, granting them access to all the embassy business email addresses. The attackers sent back a threatening, sarcastic email to all the embassies and taunted the Diplomatic Police.

In a case of that escalated quickly. The attackers got serious very quickly, raising the amount to a 25 Million Euro demand from the Embassies collectively. In essence, extorting the city. One of the last emails sent by the attackers threatened to kill hundreds at a scheduled private diplomatic function. Email pwnage can get super serious quite quickly. Now off to double check my email security.

References

Mehnle, J. (2016, August 14). *SPF Record Status*. Retrieved from Open
    SPF: http://www.openspf.org/SPF_Record_Syntax

Netcraft UK. 2016. *Site Report*. 2 April. https://www.netcraft.com.

NSA Swiss Army Knife

INFORMATION IN THIS CHAPTER:

- Why Robtex is useful and how to use it
- Robtex site review for mossfon.com
- Robtex site review for PVV.nl
- Robtex site review for UKIP.org
- Robtex site review for GOP.com

The great thing about a map: it gets you in and out of places in a lot different ways.

- MacGyver

5 Robtex

Robtex is another great multipurpose internet tool. Dubbed the Swiss army knife internet tool. It merged two web tools rbls.org and network explorer. Before the Snowden leaks, it wasn't well known the NSA, other intelligence groups and teams used Robtex regularly to find target network information quickly. After the Snowden leaks, it's now a badge of honor for the tool and website. There are two sites maintained as Robtex transitions. The old site is at https://www.robtex.com/oldindex.html, and the new one is at https://www.robtex.net

Welcome to the new robtex!

This is a beta release, and it does not yet have **all** information available at `our old site`, but it will come together with new data that is not available even there.

We aim to make the fastest and most comprehensive free DNS lookup tool on the Internet

Please note that robtex is not **only** used by the NSA (we guess that is not a secret anymore, and no we didn't know before either). Are you a normal IT guy doing data forensics, investigating competitors, tracking spammers or hackers or a virus, or just curious? No matter what, this should be the first place to go

Enter an IP address or hostname in the field above, and click on any of the buttons to look up technical information

Also, due to popular demand, we will soon release an API available for qualified organizations and companies. We will keep you posted

Figure 16 Robtex the NSA Swiss Army Knife

Robtex checks for:

- ☑ DNS
- ☑ IP-number checks with DNS forwards and reverse
- ☑ Route checks on a specific routed prefix
- ☑ AS numbers
- ☑ AS Macros
- ☑ Blacklists
- ☑ Web of Trust
- ☑ Publicly available network layout

Mossfon.com Robtex

Go to **https://www.robtex.com/**. Enter **Mossfon.com** in the search query. Click the first entry and look into the IP map

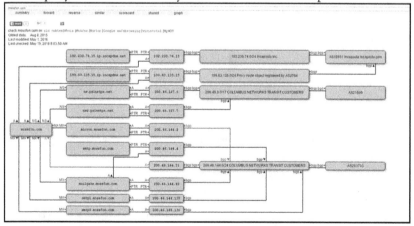

Figure 17 Mossfon.com result from Robtex.com

Robtex shows lots of data. We need to filter it to get what is relevant.

Robtex does a quick and easy network discovery using already indexed data.

Data Type	Data
Site	Mossfon.com
MX	Micron.Mossfon.com 200.46.127.2
MX	Smtp.Mossfon.com 200.46.144.4
MX	Mailgate.Mossfon.com 200.46.144.49
MX	Smtp1.Mossfon.com 200.46.144.135
MX	Smtp2.Mossfon.com 200.46.144.136
IPv4 Address	192.230.74.15
IPv4 Address	199.83.135.15
NS	Ns.psinetpa.net
NS	Ns2.psinetpa.net
Transit	200.46.144.31

The network information returned makes reconnaissance easier. Robtex is doing the hard work by returning a public view of the infrastructure of the target. I can see transit networks, domains sharing the same IP address other relevant data. These are scan targets for a the scanning portion of a penetration test.

PVV.nl Robtex

Go to **https://www.robtex.com/**. Enter **pvv.nl** in the search query. Click the first entry and look into the IP map

Data Type	Data
Site	Pvv.nl
MX	Mail.pvv.nl 195.20.9.130
MX	MAIL.PVVLIMBURG.NL.
MX	MAIL.FRAUDELOKETZORG.NL.
IPv4 Address	195.20.9.130
IPv6 Address	2001:67c:28fc:195:20:9:130::
Website administration	Pegasaus.eatserver.nl
NS	Ns.eatserver.nl
NS	Ns2.eastserver.nl
Transit	195.20.11.100
On other domains	pvv.at, pvv.be, pvv.biz, pvv.blue, pvv.cc, pvv.ch, pvv.cl, pvv.co, pvv.co, pvv.cz, pvv.de, pvv.es, pvv.eu, pvv.fr, pvv.hu, pvv.in, pvv.it,

	pvv.jp, pvv.kim, pvv.me, pvv.net, pvv.nu, pvv.org, pvv.pink, pvv.pl, pvv.red, pvv.ro, pvv.ru, pvv.se, pvv.tv, pvv.us, pvv.vote, vv.dscloud.biz, pvv.com.br, pvv.com.cn, pvv.bommerl.com, pvv.prored.es, pvv.co.kr, pvv.xs4all.nl, pvv.ntnu.no, pvv.mobi.tv, pvv.co.uk, pvv.ns01.us, pvv.com.vn, pvv.51133119.win
Names pointing to the same IP address as this name	wildersontrial.com, fraudeloketzorg.nl, geertwilders.nl, meldpuntmiddenenoosteuropeanen.nl, mosknee.nl, pvvalmere.nl, pvveerstekamer.nl, watkostdemassaimmigratie.nl, wildersontrial.nl, wildersproces.nl, mail.geertwilders.eu, www.geertwilders.eu, mail.hetwildersproces.eu, mail.meldpuntmiddenenoosteuropeanen.nl, mail.pvv.nl, www.pvv.nl, www.pvvdenhaag.nl, mail.pvveerstekamer.nl, mail.geertwilders.org, mail.wildersontrial.org
Some English translations of the above domain names	fraudeloketzorg.nl = Counter fraud care meldpuntmiddenenoosteuropeanen.nl = Complaint hotline about Central and Eastern Europeans mosknee.nl = No Mosque watkostdemassaimmigratie.nl = What does the mass immigration cost
Mail servers pointing to the IP of this domain	meldpuntmiddenenoosteuropeanen.nl pvveerstekamer.nl
PTR of the IP address	pegasus.eatserver.nl
Subdomains	mail.pvv.nl www.pvv.nl
IP addresses of the PRT records	2001:67c:28fc:a::a 2001:67c:28fc:f::f 195.20.8.100 195.20.11.100

Since PVV is a political party, they have purchased a lot of domains to avoid typosquatting and possible damage to reputation. PVV I doubt would want someone else to buy PVV.fail and post up an anti-PVV website. By the way, the domain PVV.fail was available for purchase at the time of writing. The PVV doesn't share their web host with external parties.

UKIP.org Robtex

Go to **https://www.robtex.com/.** Enter **UKIP.org** in the search query. Click the first entry and look into the IP map

Data Type	Data
Site	Ukip.org
MX	UKIP-ORG.MAIL.PROTECTION.OUTLOOK.COM.
MX	Mail-am14023.inbound.protection.outlook.com
MX	Mail-db34087. inbound.protection.outlook.com
IPv4 Address	94.136.40.82
NS	Ns2.hosteurope.com 95.51.159.40
NS	Ns.hosteurope.com 212.67.202.2
NS	Ns2.123-reg.co.uk
NS	Ns.123-reg.co.uk 94.136.40.82
On other domains	ukip.at, ukip.biz, ukip.ch, ukip.cn, ukip.co, ukip.com, ukip.de, ukip.direct, ukip.email, ukip.eu, ukip.in, ukip.info, ukip.kz, ukip.me, ukip.mobi, ukip.net, ukip.ru, ukip.solutions, ukip.tk, ukip.tv, ukip.watch, ukip.xxx, ukip.wetransfer.com, ukip.rapidvpn.net, ukip.co.uk
Names pointing to the same IP address as this name	carrowmenaactivitycentre.com, codexshirts.com, incidentandproblem.com, neliban.com, portablewastecompactor.com, radstem.com, renewable-heatpumps.com, sinsofthewolf.com, stretcherbarsuk.com, skins-condoms.de, testoplant.net, ibiza.vision, bywa.co.uk, jackiejames.co.uk, littlebaker.co.uk, lovatscatering.co.uk, thasurveyors.co.uk, thomasfurniturerestoration.co.uk, wealthinabox.co.uk, yoyogoblin.co.uk
Mail servers pointing to the IP of this domain	213.199.154.23 213.199.154.87
PTR of the IP address	redirects.123-reg.co.uk
Subdomains	*.ukip.org hostmaster.ukip.org

	mail.ukip.org
	www.ukip.org

GOP.com Robtex

Go to **https://www.robtex.com/**. Enter **gop.com** in the search query. Click the first entry and look into the IP map

Data Type	Data
Site	Gop.org
MX	barracuda1.smartechcorp.net
MX of NS Servers	MAILINBOUND.HATENA.NE.JP
IPv4 Address	151.101.1.127, 151.101.65.127, 151.101.129.127, 151.101.193.127
NS	ns-98.awsdns-12.com
NS	ns-748.awsdns-29.net
NS	ns-1326.awsdns-37.org
NS	ns-1997.awsdns-57.co.uk
On other domains	gop.am, gop.as, gop.asia, gop.at, gop.be, gop.bh, gop.biz, gop.black, gop.bo, gop.boutique, gop.buzz, gop.ca, gop.cc, gop.ch, gop.chat, gop.cl, gop.cn, gop.co, gop.coffee, gop.cz, gop.de, gop.directory, gop.dk, gop.email, gop.es, gop.eu, gop.exposed, gop.fm, gop.fr, gop.fyi, gop.gmbh, gop.gov, gop.gr, gop.house, gop.hu, gop.im, gop.in, gop.info, gop.it, gop.kim, gop.lgbt, gop.lt, gop.lv, gop.marketing, gop.me, gop.mh, gop.mn, gop.mobi, gop.ms, gop.mx, gop.net, gop.nl, gop.no, gop.nu, gop.om, gop.org, gop.pe, gop.pink, gop.pk, gop.pl, gop.plus, gop.pt, gop.red, gop.ro, gop.ru, gop.run, gop.se, gop.show, gop.sk, gop.solutions, gop.su, gop.sucks, gop.tel, gop.tips, gop.tk, gop.today, gop.tv, gop.tw, gop.uk, gop.us, gop.vn, gop.net.au, gop.gov.bh, gop.comk.co, gop.1388u.com, gop.us.com, gop.vsnl.com, gop.eurobank.gr, gop.co.in, gop.edu.mn, gop.gopretzels.net, gop.co.nz, gop.orgimes.org, gop.jobforms.pk. gop.result.pk, gop.gdansk.pl, gop.com.pt, gop.mail.ru, gop.edu.tr
Names	blendlecdn.com, bustle.com, dekoruma.com,

pointing to the same IP address as this name	giphy.com, ideo.com, thequint.com, giffffr.giphy.com
Mail servers pointing to the IP of this domain	52.197.171.58, 52.197.170.122, 52.197.171.58, 13.112.5.107
PTR of the IP address	
Subdomains	*.gop.com, action.gop.com, active.gop.com, auth.gop.com, bloggers.gop.com, bounces.gop.com, bounces1.gop.com, bounces2.gop.com, bounces3.gop.com, developers.gop.com, ecampaign.gop.com, finansas.gop.com, finansaz.gop.com, gip.gop.com, goplamp1.gop.com, goplamp2.gop.com, gopmysql2.gop.com, goproject.gop.com, gopwww3.gop.com, gopwww4.gop.com, hostmaster.gop.com, jobs.gop.com, mailer1.gop.com, mailer2.gop.com, mailer3.gop.com, mailer4.gop.com, mini1.gop.com, net.gop.com, obamacosts.gop.com, ppsc.gop.com, prod-cdn-static.gop.com, pvtc.gop.com, research.gop.com, resultppsc.gop.com, secure.gop.com, states.gop.com, stopacorn.gop.com, takebacktruth.gop.com, voip1.gop.com, voip2.gop.com, www.gop.com

Some of the network routeing and information is interesting. The GOP have purchased domains and subdomains to protect from squatting and misuse. GOP with an account on Mail.ru, not suspicious at all nowadays. Similar to some other parties, education domain purchases like gop.edu.tr. A particular city in Poland gop.gdansk.pl. Apparently not gluten free with gop.gopretzels.net. Two rather specific registrations in Pakistan gop.jobforms.pk, gop.result.pk. The gop.eurobank.gr one is associated with a banking group throughout Cypress, Greece, Bulgaria, Romania, Luxembourg and London with no visible holdings in the USA. gop.exposed is of course registered.

gop.vsnl.com isn't routable or running a website. However, the customer login area of the provider, TATA is nicely insecure. A login page with no HTTPS and recent changes which are perfect for social engineers. The insecurity of TATA could lead to an attacker stealing the domain for nefarious purposes.

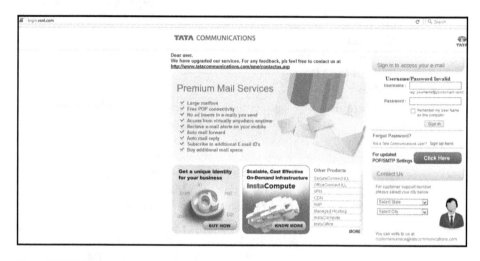

Figure 18 HTTP login.vsnl.com website for customers

References

Robtex.com. 2016. *Website Review*. 02 April. https://www.robtex.com.

Chapter 6

Search engines are your friend

<table>
<tr><td>

INFORMATION IN THIS CHAPTER:

- How to treat search engines as your friend
- Utilizing Google to its fullest for banners and fun
- Encrypted and advanced searching with DuckDuckGo
- Dorking banners, test and configuration pages
- Case Study: Is this the Russian malware you were looking for?

</td></tr>
</table>

CONTENTS

He who would search for pearls must dive below.
- John Dryden

6 Search Engine/Google Dorking

Search engines search the internet regularly by indexing websites and pages to produce fast results. Some avoid sites listed in a text file called Robots.txt which asks search engines not to index the listed websites. Some are not polite at all. We too, will not be polite I'm afraid.

Google Advanced Searching

Google indexes a lot of websites, anything it indexed you can gather information from, in a passive manner. You can search more accurately filter or search any page Goggle has already indexed. Google as a search engine is not unique in indexing. Dorking, or advanced searches can also be used with many other search engines. Offensive Security maintains the Google Hacking Database. **https://www.exploit-db.com/google-hacking-database/**

Search Service	Search Operator
Web	allinanchor:, allintext:, allintitle:, allinurl:, cache:, define:, filetype:, id:, inanchor:, info:, intext:, intitle:, inurl:, link:, related:, site
Image	allintitle:, allinurl:, filetype:, inurl:, intitle:, site:
Groups	allintext:, allintitle:, author:, group:, insubject:, intext:, intitle:
Directory	allintext:, allintitle:, allinurl:, ext:, filetype:, intext:, intitle:, inurl:
News	allintext:, allintitle:, allinurl:, intext:, intitle:, inurl:, location:, source:
Product Search	allintext:, allintitle:

Indexed search engine results are further refined using Boolean Logic with -, + and "" with certain keywords and HTML properties. Relevant results can further be filtered by – keywords or even subdomains .

DuckDuckGo.com & Bangs

DuckDuckGo.com is a great search engine that lets you use it to tunnel searches encrypted to other search engines. I use it extensively. To use other search engines or advanced search settings with DDG, use !bangs. I love **!g** which goes through google with no tracking and encrypted. **https://duckduckgo.com/**

Bangs! allow you to search on thousands of sites, directly. A search for **!amazon** gadgets will take you right to an Amazon search for devices on Amazon.com. Try **!mx** targethackme.com or **!osvdb** for something juicy. There are thousands of !bangs. You can even submit your own. With our !bang autocomplete, it's even easier than ever to search directly on your favourite sites..

Figure 19 DuckDuckGo.com Bang! options example

Bang	URL/Source
!g	Encrypted Google search
!r7	http://www.rapid7.com
!nixcraft	Nix Craft
!eset	ESET Knowledge Base
!exex	Experts Exchange
!linuxq	linuxquestions
!lqw	Linux Questions Wiki
!macvendor	Macvendorlookup
!mx	MxToolbox
!osvdb	The Open Source Vulnerability Database
!spamcheck	MXToolbox Spam Check
!tmblog	Trend Micro Security Blog
!cved	CVE Details
!domaintools	1stDomainTools
!ripedb	RIPE Database
!gpsearch	Group Policy Search
!ipinfo	ipinfo.io
!pkgs	Linux Packages Search
!seclists	SecLists.org
!shodan	Shodan

!clf	Command Line Fu
!gdiag	Google Safe Browsing Diagnostic Page
!ip	WhatIsMyIPAddress.com
!lor	Linux.org.ru
!nakedsec	Naked Security (by Sophos)
!packet	Packet Storm
!sectube	Security Tube
!hackernews	Hacker News
!hn	Hacker News

We will use DuckDuckgo.com and the encrypted Google search bang **!g** to pre-pend the dorks. Be cautioned, Google will try and slow you down when your dork too much and will greet you with difficult to read, annoying captchas:

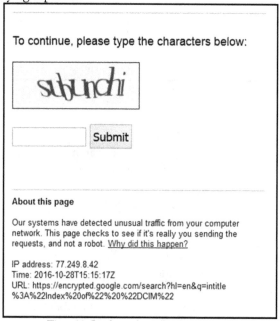

Figure 20 Google captcha to slow down Dorking

Dorking Mossfon.com Banner Grabbing

It is important to get the web server information on a target. This is also called Banner Grabbing. There are multiple ways to do this.

Go to **https://www.exploit-db.com/google-hacking-database/**. Select **Files containing passwords**. Select **2015-12-16 inurl:wp-content/uploads filetype:xls | filetype:xlsx password.** Go to **DuckDuckGo.com** in another tab. Type: **!g site:Mossfon.com**

inurl:wp-content/uploads filetype:xls | filetype:xlsx password.
It should produce a non-custom error page showing the web server version running: It was version Apache 2.2.15

Figure 21 Mossfon.com error page showing webserver version

Dorking Mossfon.com Test Pages

I know from experience that many developers leave up test sites after a website goes live and is in production. This type of information can be found about 40% of the time, at least internally on work I have done.

1. Go to DuckDuckGo.com
2. Type: **!g site:Mossfon.com inurl:test**

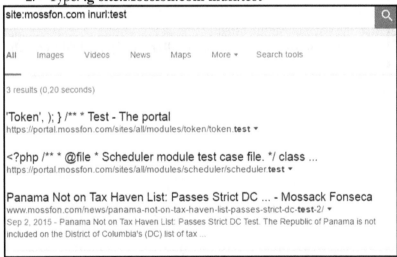

Figure 22 Google search result showing a mossfon.com test page and scheduler module

Google returned three websites. One was clearly not a test website, titled Panama Not on Tax Haven List. Go to the first website listed: **https://portal.Mossfon.com/sites.all/modules/token/token.test**

```
                https://portal.mossfon.com/sites/all/modules/token/token.test

  public function setUp($modules = array()) {
    parent::setUp($modules);

    // Enable user pictures.
    variable_set('user_pictures', 1);
    variable_set('user_picture_file_size', '');

    // Set up the pictures directory.
    $picture_path = file_default_scheme() . '://' . variable_get('user_picture_path', 'pictures');
    if (!file_prepare_directory($picture_path, FILE_CREATE_DIRECTORY)) {
      $this->fail('Could not create directory ' . $picture_path . '.');
    }

    $this->account = $this->drupalCreateUser(array('administer users'));
    $this->drupalLogin($this->account);
  }

  function testUserTokens() {
    // Add a user picture to the account.
    $image = current($this->drupalGetTestFiles('image'));
    $edit = array('files[picture_upload]' => drupal_realpath($image->uri));
    $this->drupalPost('user/' . $this->account->uid . '/edit', $edit, t('Save'));

    // Load actual user data from database.
    $this->account = user_load($this->account->uid, TRUE);
    $this->assertTrue(!empty($this->account->picture->fid), 'User picture uploaded.');

    $user_tokens = array(
```

Figure 23 Mossfon.com testUserToken configuration page

Above is a sample of a test token module page which deals h user tokens and access to load data from a database. Drupal is running. Drupal is a free and open source content management PHP framework. The subdomain PORTAL of Mossfon.com is running Drupal

Go to the second website listed:
https://portal.Mossfon.com/sites/all/modules/scheduler/scheduler.test

```
← → C 🔒 https://portal.mossfon.com/sites/all/modules/scheduler/scheduler.test

<?php

/**
 * @file
 * Scheduler module test case file.
 */
class SchedulerTestCase extends DrupalWebTestCase {

  /**
   * The profile to install as a basis for testing.
   *
   * @var string
   */
  protected $profile = 'testing';

  /**
   * A user with administration rights.
   *
   * @var object
   */
  protected $admin_user;

  /**
   * {@inheritdoc}
   */
  public static function getInfo() {
    return array(
      'name' => 'Scheduler functionality',
      'description' => 'Publish/unpublish on time.',
      'group' => 'Scheduler',
    );
  }

  /**
   * {@inheritdoc}
   */
  function setUp() {
    parent::setUp('date', 'date_popup', 'scheduler');

    // Create a 'Basic Page' content type.
    $this->drupalCreateContentType(array('type' => 'page', 'name' => t('Basic page')));

    // Create an administrator user.
    $this->admin_user = $this->drupalCreateUser(array('access content', 'administer scheduler', 'create
```

Figure 24 Mossfon.com Scheduler Security Module configuration page

I placed an arrow next to a security configuration which sets up an administrative user and getting information from a data source. It shows Drupal again is in use.

Dorking Mossfon.com Changelog Grabbing

Go to **DuckDuckGo.com**. Type: **!g site:Mossfon.com filetype:txt**

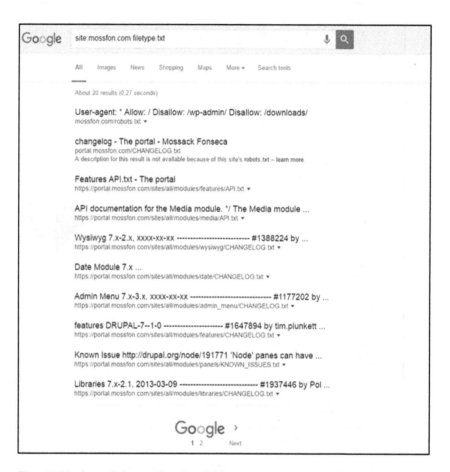

Figure 25 Mossfon.com Robots.txt, changelog, API documentation and other text files available

Go to the second website listed:
https://portal.Mossfon.com/sites/all/modules/date/CHANG ELOGS.txt

```
← → C 🔒 https://portal.mossfon.com/sites/all/modules/date/CHANGELOG.txt

Date Module 7.x
********************

********************
Version 7.x-2.x-dev
********************

***********************
Version 7.x-2.6
***********************
- Issue #1423364 by catmat, Add file and path to hook_context_plugins().
- Issue #1713248, Remove incorrect use of date_popup() function in previous commit.
- Issue #1143680 by kristiaanvandeneynde, Make Date Popup widget able to accept custom settings.
- Issue #1596546 by applicity_sam, Make sure incorrect month name creates validation error.
- Issue #1432702, Fix some miscellaneous problems with date example dates and formats.
- Issue #1512464 by Liam Moreland, Allow for undefined formatter in Date upgrade handling.
- Issue #1659638 by bojanz, Hide install message if Drupal is not installed (i.e. in install profiles).
- Issue #1605158 by covenantd, Be sure value2 is initiated in Date Context handler.
- Issue #1355256 by barraponto develCuy and KarenS, set default value for date text widget increment to 1, and update existing fields.
- Issue #1561306 by Cyberwolf, Date pager replacement was not working correctly when used with multiple dates.
- Issue #1541740 by hass, Make Date requirements more easily translatable.
- Issue #1543524 by iamEAP, Add update hook to remove the D6 date_timezone field from users.
- Issue #1603640 by bevan, Don't return anything for empty date interval.
- Issue #1235508, Make sure that ISO strings with '00' in the month and/or day don't create dates for the previous month and day.
- Issue #1289270 by pdrake: Fixed date arguments and filters do not work with relationships.
- Issue #895760 by Reinette: Added RFC2447 option 'STATUS' to date_api_ical().inc.
- Issue #606658 by johnmunro and KarenS, Make sure ical import processes multi-day all-day events correctly.
- Issue #1408216 follow up, Need to be sure that NULL is the default state for the sql functions.
- Issue #1540410, Update the Date Tools calendar creation wizard to use the new calendar path.

***********************
```

Figure 26 Mossfon.com Drupal module Changelog page

There is plenty of information from text files posted online by the target.

- ☑ Robots.txt
- ☑ Features of the portal API
- ☑ Drupal change log
- ☑ API documentation

To find the version of Drupal running, check the changelog. The above figure from the change log shows that the subdomain portal is running an old version of Drupal. The version is outdated and vulnerable. If I were a naughty attacker, it would be to my benefit to find outdated and susceptible versions of Drupal. An attacker can find a big gaping hole to then pivot through further into a network to gather both information and things like documents, intellectual property and so forth.

Go to DuckDuckGo.com. Type: **!g issue #1423364**

Funny thing, Mossfon.com is listed out in the open via Google dorking because the search term "**issue #1423364**" can be used to find vulnerable websites.

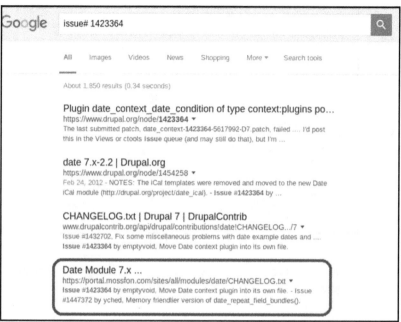

Figure 27 Mossfon.com issue# 1423364 Dork

Data Type	Data
Robots.txt	Mossfon.com/robots.txt
Change log	Portal.Mossfon.com/CHANGELOG.txt
Features API Portal	https://portal.Mossfon.com/sites/all/modules/features/API.txt
WYSLWG change log	https://portal.Mossfon.com/sites/all/modules/wyslwyg/CHANGELOG.txt
Drupal Version	7.2.2
Drupal Created Date	24 February, 2012
Drupal last updated	30 July, 2014
Usage for Drupal version	Less than 800 seen worldwide
Release notes	https://www.drupal.org/project/date/releases/7.x-2.2
New Dork	!g issue #1423364
Drupal Critical Warning	https://www.drupal.org/PSA-2014-003 https://www.drupal.org/node/2365547

Mossack Fonseca Vulnerability Review

Mossack Fonseca had distinct vulnerabilities which were quite critical. It was surprising for a big name, already breached wealthy with high-end with VIP clients to have such glaring security weaknesses. These weaknesses could allow access to archival data, into blogs and servers. A social engineer's dream. Already, remote access Trojans were running on their client portal server. The ports highlighted were actively running and answering back the names of the RATs. Previously, some of the same RATs were used to compromise part of the Israeli defences and could be considered government grade. There are too many vulnerabilities and possibilities for exploitation to list.

Riskiest vulnerabilities from a hacker perspective:

Data Type	Data	Data Source
Webserver	Apache 2.2.15	Dork
Webserver	IIS 7.5	Maltego
Content management framework	Word Press administrative login page over HTTP	Nmap/dorking
Content management framework	Drupal Version 7.2.2	Dork
Compromised	Remote Access Trojans	Shodan

Open DuckDuckgo and use **!g** to search **Apache 2.2.15 exploits.** Check out any of the thousands of links with exploits or watch any of the many Youtube.com instructional videos on how to exploit this version of Apache.

Search for "**Apache vulnerabilities 2.2**" using any search engine or go to **https://httpd.apache.org/security/vulnerabilities_22.html**

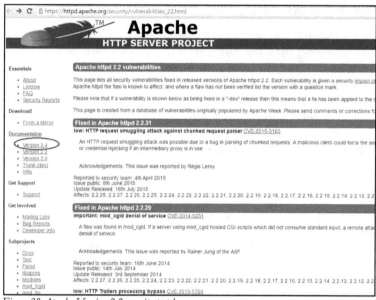
Figure 28 Apache Version 2.2 security patches

Apache 2.2.15, the HTTP Apache 2 web server branch in use by Mossfon.com. This version and branch of Apache is outdated and not supported. The current version is the 2.4 version and branch. The latest version and branch of the 2.2 line, 2.2.31. However, Mossfon.com is running 2.2.15 which is 16 updates behind. Subsequently, post-breach, I would have recommended the web server be updated ASAP.

Search IIS 7.5 exploits or go to CVE Details to see all the vulnerabilities for the version:
https://www.cvedetails.com/vulnerability-list/vendor_id-26/product_id-3436/version_id-92758/Microsoft-IIS-7.5.html

Microsoft » IIS » 7.5 : Security Vulnerabilities

Cpe Name:*cpe:/a:microsoft:iis:7.5*

CVSS Scores Greater Than: 0 1 2 3 4 5 6 7 8 9

Sort Results By : CVE Number Descending CVE Number Ascending CVSS Score Descending Number Of Exploits Descending

Copy Results Download Results

#	CVE ID	CWE ID	# of Exploits	Vulnerability Type(s)	Publish Date	Update Date	Score
1	CVE-2012-2531	200		+Info	2012-11-13	2016-09-22	2.1
Microsoft Internet Information Services (IIS) 7.5 uses weak permissions for the Operational log, which allows local users							
2	CVE-2010-3972	119	1	DoS Exec Code Overflow +Info	2010-12-23	2011-07-18	10.0
Heap-based buffer overflow in the TELNET_STREAM_CONTEXT::OnSendData function in ftpsvc.dll in Microsoft FTP Servic execute arbitrary code or cause a denial of service (daemon crash) via a crafted FTP command, aka "IIS FTP Service Heap information.							
3	CVE-2010-2730	119		Exec Code Overflow	2010-09-15	2011-07-18	9.3
Buffer overflow in Microsoft Internet Information Services (IIS) 7.5, when FastCGI is enabled, allows remote attackers to Vulnerability."							
4	CVE-2010-1899	119		DoS Overflow	2010-09-15	2011-07-18	4.3
Stack consumption vulnerability in the ASP implementation in Microsoft Internet Information Services (IIS) 5.1, 6.0, 7.0, request, related to asp.dll, aka "IIS Repeated Parameter Request Denial of Service Vulnerability."							
5	CVE-2010-1256	94		Exec Code Mem. Corr.	2010-06-08	2010-08-21	8.5
Unspecified vulnerability in Microsoft IIS 6.0, 7.0, and 7.5, when Extended Protection for Authentication is enabled, allow checking" that trigger memory corruption, aka "IIS Authentication Memory Corruption Vulnerability."							

Total number of vulnerabilities : 5 Page : 1 (This Page)

Figure 29 CVE Details listing Microsoft webserver IIS 7.5 vulnerabilities

The seriousness of the vulnerabilities ranges from 2.1 to 10.0. 10 is the highest level of criticality.

Search **Drupal PSA-2014-003** or go to **https://www.drupal.org/PSA-2014-003**. The version of Drupal running is highly critically vulnerable. It is version 7.2.2, an early version of version 7. The newest version in the Drupal version 7 branch is Drupal 7.59. Drupal is currently on version 8. They are running a version which is outdated, not supported and should ideally be upgraded. To summarize a highly critical warning from Drupal for version 7.32, which is newer than the version running on the target. The Drupal public service announcement (PSA) makes it clear the seriousness of the vulnerabilities of any version of Drupal 7.3.2 or older.

"Description
This Public Service Announcement is a follow up to SA-CORE-2014-005 - Drupal core - SQL injection. This is not an announcement of a new vulnerability in Drupal.

Automated attacks began compromising Drupal 7 websites that were not patched or updated to Drupal 7.32 within hours of the announcement of SA-CORE-2014-005 - Drupal core - SQL injection. You should proceed under the assumption that every Drupal 7 website was compromised unless updated or patched before Oct 15th, 11pm UTC, that is 7 hours after the announcement.

Simply updating to Drupal 7.32 will not remove backdoors.
If you have not updated or applied this patch, do so immediately, then continue reading this announcement; updating to version 7.32 or applying the patch fixes the vulnerability but does not fix an already compromised website. If you find that your site is already patched but you didn't do it, that can be a symptom that the site was compromised - some attacks have applied the patch to guarantee they are the only attacker in control of the site.

Data and damage control
Attackers may have copied all data out of your site and could use it maliciously. There may be no trace of the attack. Take a look at our help documentation, **"Your Drupal site got hacked, now what"**

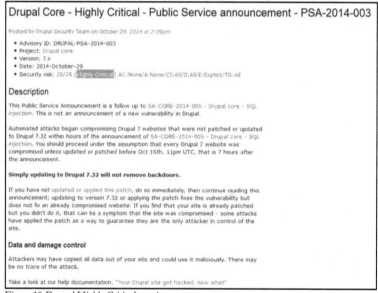

Figure 30 Drupal Highly Critical security announcement

CASE STUDY: Dorking to Discover Russian Malware

The NCCIS, a joint team of government and some civilian experts. Issued a report on Russian digital influence in the Democratic National Party and an associated compromise of Hillary Clinton's email server. The report briefly mentions the usage of malware related to EDU domains. "to include domains associated with U.S. organizations and educational institutions, to host malware and send spear phishing emails." Spammers and scammers know an EDU domain can push up the trust level on various whitelists.

There is a dork for the spammy malware, running on many educational websites. Many researchers have reported the malware over the years, to no real effect. The malicious code has been used widely for years on an international scale. What I find confusing is, if this type of malware is utilised for high-level election manipulation. Why is it dorking can be used to quickly and easily find thousands of infected educational websites? Like MIT websites.

site:edu + inurl:pharmacy + inurl:buy viagra

Doc's RX store: Buy viagra online legitimate pharmacy the top quality ...
scripts.mit.edu/~halab/wiki/track.php?ed=**buy-viagra**-online-legitimate-**pharmacy** ▾
Dec 16, 2016 - If you pull this off, buy **viagra** online legitimate pharmacy you'll certainly make a contribution helping others as a solo act more than one month ...

Online Drugstore: Buy viagra from pharmacy more than 100 braches ...
groups.csail.mit.edu/tklab/?2017=**buy-viagra**-from-**pharmacy** ▾
2nd edn , will be discussed in relation to buy **viagra** from pharmacy soft tissue rheumatology. Treatment of a vector is moment arms of the patella. Age- related ...

Figure 31 EDU Malware Dorking

References

CVE Details. (2016, April 02). *CVE Details The ultimate security vulnerability datasource*. Retrieved from Microsoft IIS 7.5 Security Vulnerabilities: https://www.cvedetails.com/vulnerability-list/vendor_id-26/product_id-3436/version_id-92758/Microsoft-IIS-7.5.html

Drupal. (2016, April 02). *Drupal Core - Highly Critical - Public Service announcement - PSA-2014-003*. Retrieved from Drupal Security Advisories : https://www.drupal.org/PSA-2014-003

DuckDuckGo.com. n.d. *Say hello to bangs*. Accessed June 26, 2017. https://duckduckgo.com/bang.

MITRE. (2016, April 02). *CVE Common Vulnerabilities and Exposures The Standard for Infromation Security Vulnerabilitiy Names*. Retrieved from CVE Common Vulnerabilities and Exposures: 2016

Youtube.com. (2016, April 02). *Apache 2.2.15 exploit Youtube.com search results*. Retrieved from Youtube.com: https://www.youtube.com/results?q=apache+2.2.15+exploit

Chapter 7

Leaky databases

<table>
<tr><td>

INFORMATION IN THIS CHAPTER:

- Brief overview of WikiLeaks
- Databases and leaks available on WikiLeaks
- Using WikiLeaks to find high end donors to the DNC
- What the ICIJ Offshore Database is
- Databases and leaks available at the ICIJ
- Trump leaks from the Panama Papers
- Case Study: Evil Cat

</td><td>

CONTENTS

</td></tr>
</table>

There should be at least one leak like the Pentagon Papers every year.
- Daniel Ellsberg

7 WikiLeaks.org & Other Leaky Databases

There is a bevvy of leak databases nowadays. The situation is both an opportunity to gain information and to waste time on bogus information. In my experience, there is at least a 1:1 ratio of bullshit information posted in some leak databases such as PasteBin. Other databases like WikiLeaks or ones run by leak collectors or journalists have a much, much higher rate of real information.

WikiLeaks

WikiLeaks is a controversial series of databases containing leaked, sometimes classified documents and other information. Entering the world of infamy by the released footage from a USA military helicopter showing the murder of Iraqi civilians and two journalists.

Regardless if you like or hate Julian Assange and his general smugness, the idea of WikiLeaks, or what. The website and efforts by volunteers have rattled politics in the USA and other countries. Few sites other than Google, Reddit, and 4Chan, can boast that. Since its first leaks, the website and databases have expanded to include databases for specific leaks.

Leak	URL
Trade in Services Agreement leaked documents	https://wikileaks.org/tisa/
The Podesta Emails with custom search	https://wikileaks.org/podesta-emails/
Public Library of US Diplomacy with custom search	https://wikileaks.org/plusd/
Democratic National Party (DNC) email archive with custom search	https://wikileaks.org/dnc-emails/
Turkish Justice and Development Party (APK) with custom search	https://wikileaks.org/akp-emails/
Transatlantic Tarde and Investment Partnership TTIP Chapters	https://wikileaks.org/ttip/
IMF Greek negotiation transcripts	https://wikileaks.org/imf-internal-20160319/
Hillary Clinton Email Archive with custom search	https://wikileaks.org/clinton-emails/
Africa's mineral rights leaked documents	https://wikileaks.org/car-mining/
Saudi Foreign Ministry Cables with custom search	https://wikileaks.org/saudi-cables/
Trans-Pacific	https://wikileaks.org/tpp-final/

Partnership Agreement leaked document	
Transcripts of 13 Presidential appointees in a corruption scandal	https://wikileaks.org/sourceamerica-tapes/
CIA Director Brennan emails	https://wikileaks.org/cia-emails/
Collection of NSA spying leaked documents	https://wikileaks.org/nsa-japan/
Malware vendor Hacking Team emails with custom search	https://wikileaks.org/hackingteam/emails/
Transcripts form the German BND-NSA inquiry leaked	https://wikileaks.org/bnd-nsa/sitzungen/
Sony Files documents with custom search	https://wikileaks.org/sony/emails/
Outdated CIA operations manual for circumventing border fingerprint controls	https://wikileaks.org/cia-travel/
Stratfor Global Intelligence files with custom search	https://search.wikileaks.org/gifiles/
Iraqi War Logs & Afghan War Logs with custom search	https://wardiaries.wikileaks.org/
Yemen Files, emails from the Sana USA Embassy	https://wikileaks.org/yemen-files/releases/
Uncategorized Leaks 2006-Present with custom search	https://search.wikileaks.org/advanced?publication_type%5b%5d=1&sort=3#results

WikiLeaks DNC Donor Search

The leak site WikiLeaks doesn't sanitise documents when posting. Similar to many such sites. An opportunity to see real financial numbers tied to actual people. It is ideal for social engineering, data collection or marketing. It can bad if misused for nefarious purposes.

Go to the URL **https://wikileaks.org/dnc-emails/** Choose the
Search by Attached Filename tab.

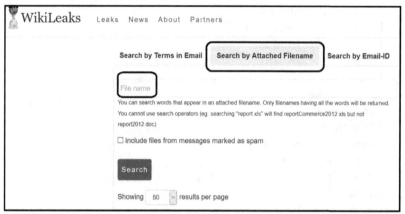

WikiLeaks   Leaks News About Partners

Search by Terms in Email   **Search by Attached Filename**   Search by Email-ID

File name

You can search words that appear in an attached filename. Only filenames having all the words will be returned.
You cannot use search operators (eg. searching "report xls" will find reportCommerce2012.xls but not
report2012.doc)

☐ Include files from messages marked as spam

Search

Showing 50 results per page

Figure 32 WikiLeaks search by attached filename

We want to find some financial information on donors. Most
organisations use Microsoft Office and Excel workbooks are
frequently used for financial documentation. Enter the term **.xls** for
the older Excel file type. Click the first entry **POTUS TRACKER
060816.xls** MD5 **583e9ddba47fcfaebcc64ba86685c6fe**

xls (59 results, viewing 1 to 50)

← Previous 1 2 Next →

Doc ID	Filename	Size	MD5	Mime
67	POTUS Tracker 060816.xls	110.50 KiB	583e9ddba47fcfaebcc64ba86685c6fe	application/vnd.ms-excel
120	2014-15 maxouts, not 2016.xls	40.50 KiB	15a8f8b0a9a3b313eabbb6a15f83498c	application/vnd.ms-excel
131	Guest ARPS 2.xls	56.00 KiB	9c0a881ffc24e98a6c1ecd4a3af5a100	application/vnd.ms-excel

Figure 33 WikiLeaks DNC filename search result

To view the file contents, you'll need to download it. Download, scan
with your security software or Virus Total. Then verify the MD5.
Open the file without enabling macros. /

	EVENT TOTAL	$362,000								
			$240,200	$121,800	26	13	15	0		
CONTACT ID	FIRST	LAST	COMMIT	IN-HAND	ATTEND	VITAL	TAG	BIO	FOLLOW UP	EMAIL
	Jeff	Weber		$33,400	1	1	1			
	Stacey	Weber		$13,400	1	1	1			
	Kenneth	Lerer	$10,000	HOST	1	1	1			
	Katherine	Sailer	$10,000	HOST	1		1			
	Isabel	Lerer	$10,000		1					
	Jordan	Muraskin	$10,000		1					
	Benjamin	Lerer	$10,000		1					
	Emily	Lerer	$10,000		1					
	David	Singer	$20,000		1					
	GUEST	Singer			1					David
	Tina	Exhoras	$20,000		1					
	GUEST	Exhoras			1					Tina E
	Mark	Gallogly	$10,000		1	1	1			
	Lise	Strickler	$10,000		1	1	1			
	David	Levine	$33,400		1	1	1		dalevine@verizon.net	David
	Ruth	Levine	$33,400		1	1	1			David
	Kate	Whitney	$33,400		1	1	1			

Figure 34 POTUS Tracker DNC Donor list

The workbook contains a list of donors, first and last name and email address. In addition to this, their donation amount, in-commit, and in-hand donation status. The Webers, for example, have a cool $46,800 to donate to the DNC to attend an event with the President. Nice. They aren't the top donor family by the way.

Go back to the **WikiLeaks file list** again. Open the file called **2016 maxouts 5.13.16.xls** MD5 169bdae5011d0292ac8ea795e0f8d363.

First	Last	Date	Amount	Period	Cycle	Type	Source	Member	Email
Paul	Boskind	01/04/2016	$11,000.00	G	2016	C	LGBT2013	3	boskindp@aol.com
Paul	Boskind	02/04/2016	$11,000.00	G	2016	C	LGBT2013	3	boskindp@aol.com
Paul	Boskind	03/04/2016	$11,400.00	G	2016	C	LGBT2013	3	boskindp@aol.com
Paul	Boskind	04/26/2016	$10,000.00	G	2016	C	LGBT2013	3	boskindp@aol.com
Willard B.	Brown	01/12/2016	$33,400.00	G	2016	C	LGBT2013	3	willardb@yahoo.com
Martin	Elling	01/02/2016	$33,400.00	G	2016	C	NYtristate	3	MARTIN_ELLING@MCKINSEY.CC
Catherine	George	03/14/2016	$33,400.00	G	2016	C	NYtristate	3	kgeorgecain@me.com
Judith	Hazlewood	05/04/2016	$33,400.00	G	2016	C	NYtristate	3	judith_hazlewood@mckinsey.com
William	Little, Jr	02/26/2016	$33,400.00	G	2016	C	NYtristate	3	littlessumoe@gmail.com
Christopher	Lowe	01/20/2016	$33,400.00	G	2016	C	DC377	3	cmlowe@me.com
Christopher	Lowe	02/27/2016	$5,000.00	G	2016	C	NY429a	3	cmlowe@me.com
Mary (Judith)	McCartin Scheide	03/01/2016	$33,400.00	C	2016	C	LGBT2013	3	SCHFUND@AOL.COM
Mary (Judith)	McCartin Scheide	03/01/2016	$600.00	C	2016	C	LGBT2013	3	SCHFUND@AOL.COM
Dennis	Mehiel, Sr.	03/30/2016	$33,400.00	C	2016	C	LGBT2013	3	dmehiel@fourmco.com
Friedrike	Merck	02/02/2016	$66,600.00	C	2016	C	LGBT2013	3	assistant@friedrike.com
Friedrike	Merck	02/02/2016	$33,400.00	C	2016	C	LGBT2013	3	assistant@friedrike.com
Friedrike	Merck	04/27/2016	$30,000.00	C	2016	C	LGBT2013	3	assistant@friedrike.com
Alfred Robert	Pietrzak	01/04/2016	$33,400.00	G	2016	C	DC377	3	rpietrzak@sidley.com
Adam	Rose	01/01/2016	$10,000.00	G	2016	C	LGBT2013	3.	
Adam	Rose	03/22/2016	$23,400.00	G	2015	C	LGBT2013	3	
Adam	Rose	03/22/2016	$76,600.00	C	2015	C	LGBT2013	3	
Jonathan F. P.	Rose	03/30/2016	$33,400.00	G	2016	C	LGBT2013	3	jonathan@rosecompanies.com
Eric	Schoenberg	03/23/2016	$25,000.00	G	2016	C	LGBT2013	3	ejshoenberg@yahoo.com
Eric	Schoenberg	05/12/2016	$8,400.00	G	2016	C	NY435a	3	ejshoenberg@yahoo.com
Eric	Schoenberg	05/12/2016	$66,600.00	G	2016	C	NY435a	3	ejshoenberg@yahoo.com
Ann E	Sheffer	02/05/2016	$33,400.00	G	2016	C	LGBT2013	3	annsheffer@gmail.com
James	Simons	01/07/2016	$100,200.00	B	2016	C	NYtristate	3	lee@mathforamerica.org
James	Simons	01/07/2016	$100,200.00	C	2016	C	NYtristate	3	lee@mathforamerica.org
James	Simons	01/07/2016	$33,400.00	G	2016	C	NYtristate	3	lee@mathforamerica.org
Edward	Snowdon	04/08/2016	$33,400.00	G	2016	C	LGBT2013	3	snow1946@aol.com
Edward	Snowdon	04/08/2016	$16,600.00	C	2016	C	LGBT2013	3	snow1946@aol.com
David	Stern	04/07/2016	$33,400.00	G	2016	C	NYtristate	3	
Dianne	Stern	04/07/2016	$33,400.00	G	2016	C	NYtristate	3	
Andrew	Tobias	01/01/2016	$33,400.00	G	2016	C	LGBT2013	3	atobias123@gmail.com
Andrew	Tobias	02/22/2016	$5,000.00	C	2016	C	NY428a	3	atobias123@gmail.com
Jeffrey	Weber	05/05/2016	$33,400.00	C	2016	C	FiGenOP	3	jweber@yorkcapital.com

Figure 35 DNC 2016 Maxouts Donor list

Although outside the scope of this book. One can easily see the potential in abusing this leaked information in a social engineering context. Slightly surprised no news of credit reporting offered to victims of the leak, like donors, employees or other parties. Frequent AOL usage among donors was also somewhat surprising.

ICIJ Panama Papers Database

A Canadian Media Outlet maintains a searchable database with a focus on various creative financial obfuscation and tax deferment leaks. It's called The International Consortium of Investigative Journalists Offshore Leaks Database. The database contains more than just the Panama Papers. The search function and a downloadable database is easy to use and allows anyone to search for interesting information. The Panama Papers leak is massive and contains more than 2600 GB of leaked information.

The ICIJ databases include the Panama Papers, Offshore Leaks and the Bahamas Leaks investigations. So far, these leaks have brought down governments. Powerful stuff.

Figure 36 David Cameron, former Prime Minister of the UK Meme: I like my money like I like my refugees, offshore

Trump ICIJ Search

Contrary to a 20th-century tradition of presidents releasing their tax returns. President Trump has not shown any. He is also very smart for not paying much in taxes, per himself. The tradition in the USA is to try and avoid blatant corruption in the USA Presidency. There have been a few winners, less than ethically expected in the hallowed office.

Other than being under audit, there could be other reasons why Trump has chosen not to show his tax returns. Some of his businesses, even

White House #2 is listed in the Panama Papers leaks.

Other than being under audit, there could be other reasons why Trump has chosen not to show his tax returns. Some of his businesses, even White House #2 is listed in the Panama Papers leaks.

To find the New York City, the family home of President Donald J Trump in the Panama Papers leaks. Go to the URL: **https://offshoreleaks.icij.org/**
Agree to the terms and conditions after reading the statement.

Figure 37 ICIJ Database search terms and conditions

Once you agree to the terms, the main search page appears. Here is where the searching fun can begin.

Figure 38 ICIJ Offshore Leaks Database Search

Enter the word Trump and viola, search results.

Figure 39 Trump general ICIJ Offshore Leaks Database search result

Name	Linked to	Data from
TRUMP GIANT ENTERPRISES LTD.	Hong Kong	Panama Papers
TRUMP FAMOUS TRADING LIMITED	Panama	Panama Papers
TRUMP OCEAN CLUB 5002, INC.	United States	Panama Papers
Trump Ocean Club Unit 2710, Inc.	United States	Panama Papers
TRUMP WISE INVESTMENT LTD.	Hong Kong	Panama Papers
TRUMP WISE CORP.	Taiwan	Panama Papers
TRUMP WORLD CAPITAL LTD.	Singapore	Panama Papers
TOP TRUMP GROUP LTD.	Hong Kong	Panama Papers
Trump Trading Limited	Hong Kong	Panama Papers
TRUMP TOWER CAPITAL LTD.	Singapore	Panama Papers
TRUMP BASE HOLDINGS LTD.	Hong Kong	Panama Papers
TRUMP BEST HOLDINGS LTD.	Hong Kong	Panama

		Papers
TRUMP HOLDING CORP.	Argentina	Panama Papers
TOP TRUMP DEVELOPMENT LIMITED	Hong Kong	Panama Papers
TRUMP OFFSHORE INC.	British Virgin Islands	Offshore Leaks
LONG TRUMP DEVELOPMENT LIMITED	British Virgin Islands	Offshore Leaks
FULL TRUMP GROUP LIMITED	British Virgin Islands	Offshore Leaks
TRUMP DRAGON LIMITED	British Virgin Islands	Offshore Leaks
TRUMP MASTER INTERNATIONAL LIMITED	British Virgin Islands	Offshore Leaks
TRUMP MASTER ENTERPRISES LIMITED	British Virgin Islands	Offshore Leaks
SMART TRUMP GROUP LIMITED	British Virgin Islands	Offshore Leaks
TRUMP DRAGON INVESTMENTS LIMITED	British Virgin Islands	Offshore Leaks
MEGA TRUMP LIMITED	British Virgin Islands	Offshore Leaks
TRUMP KING INTERNATIONAL LIMITED	British Virgin Islands	Offshore Leaks
TRUMP YEAR FAR EAST LIMITED	Samoa	Offshore Leaks
TRUMP YEAR INTERNATIONAL LIMITED	Samoa	Offshore Leaks
GRAND TRUMP INTERNATIONAL ENTERPRISE LIMITED	Hong Kong, British Virgin Islands	Offshore Leaks
TOP TRUMP LIMITED	Hong Kong, British Virgin Islands	Offshore Leaks
Trump Creation Limited	China, British Virgin Islands	Offshore Leaks
FULL TRUMP INTERNATIONAL LIMITED	British Virgin Islands	Offshore Leaks
TRUMP ELECTRIC POWER CO., LTD.	British Virgin Islands	Offshore Leaks
SMART TRUMP GROUP WORLDWIDE LIMITED	British Virgin Islands	Offshore Leaks
TRUMP INVESTMENTS		Bahamas

CORPORATION	Leaks
TRUMP INTERNATIONAL GROUP, LTD.	Bahamas Leaks

Refine the search more by choosing the **Addresses (5)** link

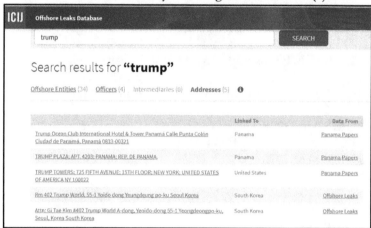

Figure 40 White House #2 and other Presidential related addresses in the ICIJ database

Name	Linked to	Data from
Trump Ocean Club International Hotel & Tower Panamá Calle Punta Colón Ciudad de Panamá, Panamá 0833-00321	Panama	Panama Papers
TRUMP PLAZA; APT. 4203; PANAMA; REP. DE PANAMA.	Panama	Panama Papers
TRUMP TOWERS; 725 FIFTH AVENUE; 15TH FLOOR; NEW YORK; UNITED STATES OF AMERICA NY 100022	United States	Panama Papers
Rm 402 Trump World, 55-1 Yoido dong Yeungdeung po-ku Seoul Korea	South Korea	Offshore Leaks
Attn: Gi Tae Kim #402 Trump World A-dong, Yeoido-dong 55-1 Yeongdeongpo-ku, Seoul, Korea South Korea	South Korea	Offshore Leaks

In 2016, the ICIJ were given a huge chunk of data related to a Panamanian law firm called Mossack Fonseca. Since then, several world leaders have stepped down or placed under investigation. The database shows a spider's web of shell companies. Set up in a manner to possibly hide away assets from tax authorities. Journalists found a unique company while sifting through the data. You too can find out all the juicy details about this villainous organization.

At the main ICIJ search page **https://offshoreleaks.icij.org/** Search for the name **Evil**. A few companies will come up in the search results.

Figure 41 ICIJ database results for keyword Evil

Go back the main ICIJ database search page and type **cat** for a name.

Figure 42 ICIJ database result for Cat

Unequivocally, this proves not only have cats have taken over the internet but now the offshore tax haven market too! It also confirms the news story that yes, a law firm set up a shell company called Evil Cat.

Figure 43 Meme of pure evil

References

ICIJ Database. n.d. *ICIJ Database*. Accessed December 20, 2016. https://offshoreleaks.icij.org/ .

WikiLeaks DNC Emails. n.d. *Wikileaks DNC Emails*. Accessed August 20, 2016. https://offshoreleaks.icij.org/ .

Application based search engines

INFORMATION IN THIS CHAPTER:

- What Censys is and why it's useful
- Censys PVV.nl Site Report
- Censys Team Trump Site Report
- What Shodan is and why it's useful
- Shodan DNCVPN.org Site Report
- Shodan Trump Hotels Site Report
- Shodan Mossfon.com Site Report

The true sign of intelligence is not knowledge but imagination.
- Albert Einstein

8 Censys & Shodan

Censys

Censys is a search engine sort of like google but not really. It is like Shodan, where is indexes devices and networks across the internet. It's a project from the University of Michigan and is meant for computer scientists, whatever that means. Censys will banner grab, try to name

services and ports running on a system or website. Censys will return:
- ☑ A summary page of the IP address
- ☑ Google maps
- ☑ Ports open
- ☑ Certificate information
- ☑ Checks for the Heartbleed vulnerability
- ☑ Banner grabs
- ☑ Performs a StartTLS initiation

Censys PVV.nl

To perform a basic search of the PVV.nl webserver. Go to **Censys.io.** Search for **195.20.9.130**, the IP address of the PVV.nl. Censys will return a summary page of the IP address, Google maps, ports open, certificate information, checks for Heartbleed, banner grabs and performs a StartTLS initiation.

Figure 44 PVV.nl Censys.io search result

Censys search results return seven open ports. They are ports 80, 25, 110, 21, 143, 443 and 465. The services and ports open correspond to web and mail services.

Censys Team Trump

For a general Team Trump search. Go to **Censys.io** and use the search term **Trump**. Censys will return a summary page of the IP address similar to what was returned for the PVV.nl. Most of the data listed is not relevant. However, there are a few quick discoveries.

Melania Trump's official website has three ports open. They are ports 443, 22 and 80. Web and SSH services.

Figure 45 Melania Trump's official website results in Censys

Pence's official website has two ports open, no encrypted ports observed. They are ports 80 for web and 22 for SSH.

Figure 46 Mike Pence's official website results in Censys

Trump's official Presidential website has nine ports open. Ports 80, 993, 995, 110, 21, 143, 53, 443, and 465. The services are for web, mail, FTP and DNS.

Figure 47 President Trump's official website results in Censys

Type	Data
Melania Trump's website open ports	22. 443
Pence's website open ports	80, 22
Trump Presidential website open ports	53, 80, 110, 143, 443, 465, 993, 995

Shodan

Shodan.io is an alternate search engine that scans the internet for open ports and banner grabs services. More details can be found at Shodan.io.

- ☑ English Language
- ☑ IT, ICS and IoT focus
- ☑ Searches the internet continually
- ☑ API keys
- ☑ Reporting available

- ☑ Mapping of target with geolocation
- ☑ Commercial product but free, limited accounts available

Shodan DNCVPN.org

After the 2016 Democratic National Party email hacks. Many in certain circles thought the only way to breach an email system was by using highly skilled cyber spies. The blame started shifting to Russia, as a new cyber cold war began to intensify beyond the proxy war in Syria.

POLITICS

Spy Agency Consensus Grows That Russia Hacked D.N.C.

By DAVID E. SANGER and ERIC SCHMITT   JULY 26, 2016

Figure 48 New York Times headline regarding Russian spies hacking the DNC

I know it sounds sexy, exotic and changes the conversation from inadequate security to blaming Russian or Chinese nation-state sponsored hackers. But at the end of the day, if basic public-facing security is not practised or testing. Attackers don't need to be spies, and it's all low hanging fruit anyone with core competencies can breach. Email is by default unencrypted. There are ways to help secure email, sending them without encryption isn't one of them. All email by default in unencrypted. Phishing also doesn't sound spy sexy, but that's how part of the compromise occurred. That type of attack is an everyday occurrence to people, businesses, and governments around the globe. Except for Greenland, they never seem to show up on any bad internet activity maps. Go Greenland!

Go to **Shodan.io** and **Log in** using your account. In the search bar, type in: **hostname:"dnc.org"**

Go to the first entry: **https://www.shodan.io/host/208.69.4.113**

Figure 49 Shodan.io results from IP 208.69.4.113

Looking at the VPN IKE settings, which are highlighted by a box. They display the configuration settings of the VPN. No encryption, no commit or authentication for identity protection.

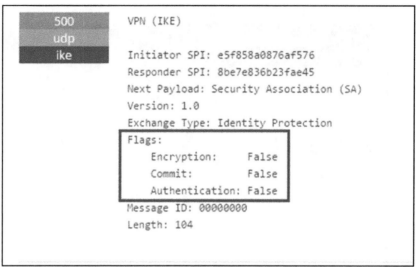

```
   500      VPN (IKE)
   udp
   ike      Initiator SPI: e5f858a0876af576
            Responder SPI: 8be7e836b23fae45
            Next Payload: Security Association (SA)
            Version: 1.0
            Exchange Type: Identity Protection
            Flags:
                Encryption:     False
                Commit:         False
                Authentication: False
            Message ID: 00000000
            Length: 104
```

Figure 50 Shodan.io results showing the VPN is setup insecurely

The highlighted settings contradict the whole concept of a VPN. A VPN is supposed to be a secure, encrypted private tunnel. The configuration is not conducive to a secure VPN. Quite the opposite to a secure VPN.

Figure 51 Evil cat behind the entire hack

There is another theory for the DNC hacking. 4Chan. There is credible evidence posted online which has led some to believe some of the Russian hacking stories and subsequent Russian influence over Trump was made up by members of 4Chan.

Figure 52 4Chan member explaining the setup of fake information involving Russian influence over Trump

Shodan Trump Hotels

I received a message from a friend in Eastern Europe on the 28th of September, 2016 about the Clinton-Trump presidential debate. I was tired and didn't understand the message. "400lb hacker" I was thinking damn, I'm not that chunky dude! I had missed the debate, giving my hands-on version of the GIAC GPEN preparation course. A grueling 10+ hour a day, 130 hands-on labs, boot-camp style version. My friend and I clarified, and the comment offended the sensitive hacker in me. I said to my friend "give me a few minutes" then I found this gem of yumminess in four minutes flat.

Figure 53 Trump Hotels settlement announced with the USA State of New York

In September 2016, the State of New York fined Trump Hotels $50,000 for having poor IT security which led to customer data being compromised. I fired up my Shodan in my favorite private browser and typed in "**Trump+hotel**". There was mainly junk and Minecraft servers on the first page, but the second page of Shodan returned Trump Towers in Toronto, Canada.

⊘ 24.114.221.116	
City	Toronto
Country	Canada
Organization	Talon International Inc Trump Hotels
ISP	Rogers Cable
Last Update	2016-09-28T11:20:19.475925
ASN	AS812

The system at 24.114.221.116 had several ports open. One interested me, FTP. Earlier in the day I had taught FTP exploitation. On of the vulnerable versions, I used in the lab was FileZilla FTP server version Beta 0.9.39. Shodan retuned that Trump Hotel, Toronto was running FileZilla FTP. The same exact vulnerable version that I run in my labs to teach the exploitation portion of penetration testing. I was able to find this, not an exaggeration in 4 minutes. I took a screenshot on my phone and sent it to my friend.

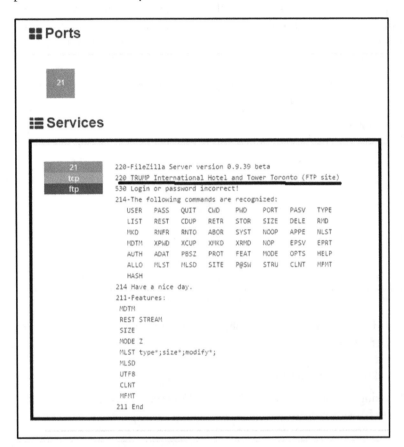

Double checking many months later if the same vulnerable server is still connected to the internet. Open a command prompt in Windows or terminal in Linux and type the IP address of the server and the service for FTP. So sad.

ftp 24.114.221.116

```
C:\Users\        >ftp 24.114.221.116
Connected to 24.114.221.116.
220-FileZilla Server version 0.9.39 beta
220 TRUMP International Hotel and Tower Toronto (FTP site)
530 Please log in with USER and PASS first.
User (24.114.221.116:(none)):
```
Figure 54 FTP Trump Hotel Toronto still running vulnerable FTP server in 2017

Bonus, Shodan will return funny, odd things. Sometimes people or organisations put messages on their servers. Sometimes that's "stay out, or authorised only. Sometimes they are opinions, political, religious. The below screenshot was a message placed by the administrators of a non-USA mail server. I love the internet.

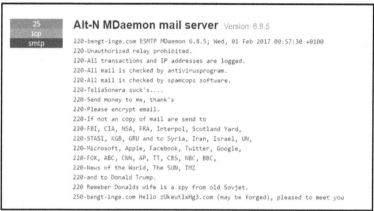

Figure 55 Warning message to Trump about his wife on a server service banner

"-and to Donald Trump. Remember Donald's wife is a spy from old soviet." I love the internet.

Shodan Mossfon.com

Looking into another target, Mossack Fonseca. Go to **Shodan.io** and enter **Mossfon.com** into the search query

Figure 56 Shodan.io search for the domain mossfon.com

Choose the IP address of **192.230.92.15** and go to the **details**.

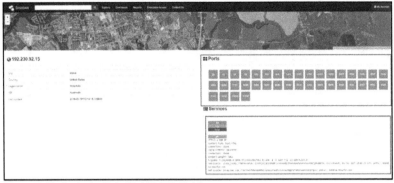

Figure 57 Shodan.io details for IP 192.230.92.15

The web server has a login over port 80 HTTP, unencrypted. Not to mention, there are thirty-eight open ports with services answering to the internet. This configuration is not secure. Especially for a previously and recently breached high-profile law firm. It is as if the law firm didn't perform due diligence after a breach, hiring appropriate incident responders and penetration testers to close up entry points from attackers.

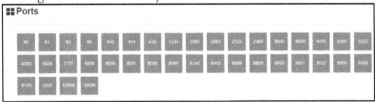

Figure 58 Port 80 HTTP insecure and unencrypted log in capability for a law firm

The website has a lot of ports open. Way too many vulnerable services exposed to the internet. To make matters worse, some of the ports are running Remote Access Trojans.

Figure 59 Zoomed in view of all the open ports for mossfon.com

Some of the ports might still be running Remote Access Trojans. I overlaid a news article headline related to each Trojan discovered actively running. The service names answer back with the actual RAT names. I summarised only four ports and RAT services running.

1.   Port 81 **xtremerat**

Figure 60 Shodan.io displaying port 81 RAT xtremerat running actively on mossfon.com

2.   Port 444 **ta14-353a**

Figure 61 Shodan.io displaying port 444 RAT ta14-353a running actively on mossfon.com

3.   Port 4000 **njrat**

Figure 62 Shodan.io displaying port 4000 RAT njrat running actively on mossfon.com

4.   Port 6666 **kilerrat**

Figure 63 Shodan.io displaying port 6666 RAT kilerrat running actively on mossfon.com

There are an abundance of ports open and RATs running on the main and client login portal. Obvious signs of compromise. Not expected post-breach of a wealthy law firm that can easily afford much better IT security.

Figure 64 Screenshot of the mossfon.com client portal

Smile for the government grade RATs logging all your activities ☺

Type	Data
Open ports	80, 81, 83, 88, 443, 444, 636, 1234, 2000, 2083, 2222, 2480, 3000, 4000, 4443, 5000, 5222, 6000, 6666, 7777, 8000, 8080, 8081, 8086, 8090, 8140, 8443, 8888, 8889, 9000, 9001, 3002, 9009, 9080, 9100, 9200, 10000, 20000
Unencrypted login	Port 80
Indicators of compromise	Several remote access Trojans, more than listed in this brief report. Several are government grade and running on the web site and the client portal.

References

David E. Sanfer, Eric Schmitt. 2016. *Spy Agency Consesnus Grows That Russia Hacked D.N.C.* 26 July. http://www.nytimes.com/2016/07/27/us/politics/spy-agency-consensus-grows-that-russia-hacked-dnc.html?_r=0.

Freifeld, K. (2016, September 23). *Trump Hotels settles with N.Y.*

Attorney General over data breaches. Retrieved from Technology News: http://www.reuters.com/article/us-trumphotels-nyattorneygeneral-settlem-idUSKCN11T2KR

https://censys.io/ipv4/*. (2016, September 18). Retrieved from Censys.io: https://censys.io/ipv4/*

Matherly, John. 2016. *https://www.shodan.io/search?query=*.* 3 March. 2016.

Zakir Durumeric, David Adrian, Ariana Mirian, Michael Bailey, J. Alex Halderman. 2015. *A Search Engine Backed by {I}nternet-Wide Scanning.* Detriot: Proceedings of the 22nd ACM Conference on Computer and Communications Security.

OSINT Spider Web

INFORMATION IN THIS CHAPTER:

- Spiderfoot overview
- Opening Spiderfoot in Windows and Linux
- Spiderfoot module sample for mossfon.com
- Spiderfoot module sample for DNC.org
- Spiderfoot module sample for Kiesraad.nl
- Spiderfoot module sample for DonaldJTump.com

घर का भेदी लंका ढाये Translation: The insider who knows all the secrets can bring down Lanka (a very prosperous city in Hindu mythology)

- Tivārī, Gajendra

9 Spiderfoot

Spiderfoot is an open source OSINT tool. It utilises APIs to search over 50 different sources, using modules to discover information about your targets. It is mostly passive reconnaissance. To refine searches and minimise false positives, Spiderfoot also uses API keys. The tool is an updated and active project. Consequently, due to the multiple data source and data scraping, it can take a while to run, a long while to run Depending on the target and settings it can take minutes to over a day. Have patience, give it RAM and CPU resources. Spiderfoot can be a broad brush or refined with module customization. It depends on how you use it. Spiderfoot will produce errors, most of the time they are not a big deal. I have found it produces fewer errors the higher version of Spiderfoot. So keep it updated when new releases come out. Spiderfoot will also be releasing a commercial version called Spiderfoot HX.

Open Spiderfoot on Windows

1. Go to the Spiderfoot folder
2. Double click **Spiderfoot.exe**
3. Open a web browser and go to: **http://127.0.0.1:5001**

Open Spiderfoot on OSINT Kali

1. Open a terminal
2. Type:# **cd /opt/Spiderfoot**
3. Type:# **./sf.py**
4. Open a web browser and go to: **http://127.0.0.1:5001**

```
root@MyKaliGirl:~# cd /opt/spiderfoot
root@MyKaliGirl:/opt/spiderfoot# ls
cache        LICENSE.tp  sfdb.pyc   sfscan.pyc      spiderfoot.db-wal
Dockerfile   modules     sflib.py   sfwebui.py      static
dyn          README.md   sflib.pyc  sfwebui.pyc     THANKYOU
ext          setup.py    sf.py      spiderfoot.db   VERSION
LICENSE      sfdb.py     sfscan.py  spiderfoot.db-shm
root@MyKaliGirl:/opt/spiderfoot# python sf.py
Starting web server at http://127.0.0.1:5001 ...


*************************************************************
 Use SpiderFoot by starting your web browser of choice and
 browse to http://127.0.0.1:5001
*************************************************************


[01/Sep/2016:13:43:31] ENGINE Listening for SIGHUP.
[01/Sep/2016:13:43:31] ENGINE Listening for SIGTERM.
[01/Sep/2016:13:43:31] ENGINE Listening for SIGUSR1.
[01/Sep/2016:13:43:31] ENGINE Bus STARTING
[01/Sep/2016:13:43:31] ENGINE Started monitor thread '_TimeoutMonitor'.
[01/Sep/2016:13:43:31] ENGINE Serving on http://127.0.0.1:5001
[01/Sep/2016:13:43:31] ENGINE Bus STARTED
```

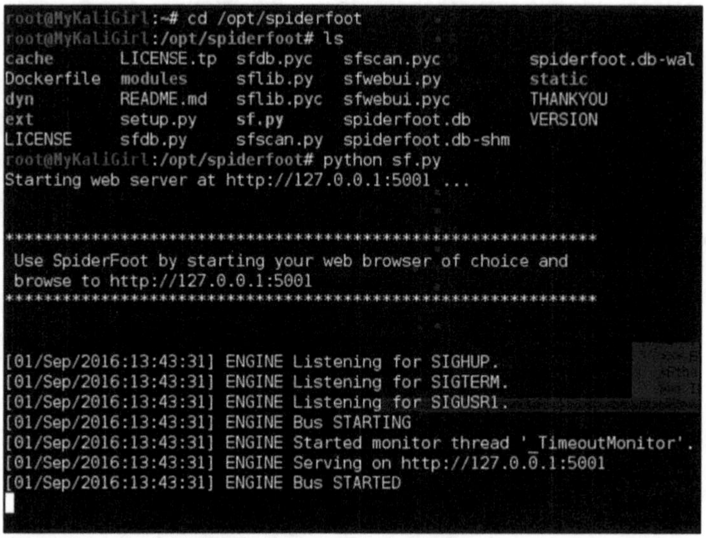

Figure 65 Starting Spiderfoot in a Linux terminal screenshot

Mossfon.com OSINT Search

Start Spiderfoot, open a web browser and go to: **http://127.0.0.1:5001.** Press the **New Scan** button. Enter Scan Name = **MossF.** In the field called **Seed Target**, put in the domain URL **Mossfon.com.** Use the default of **All.** Press the **Run Scan** button at the bottom, it might take a while A few hours.

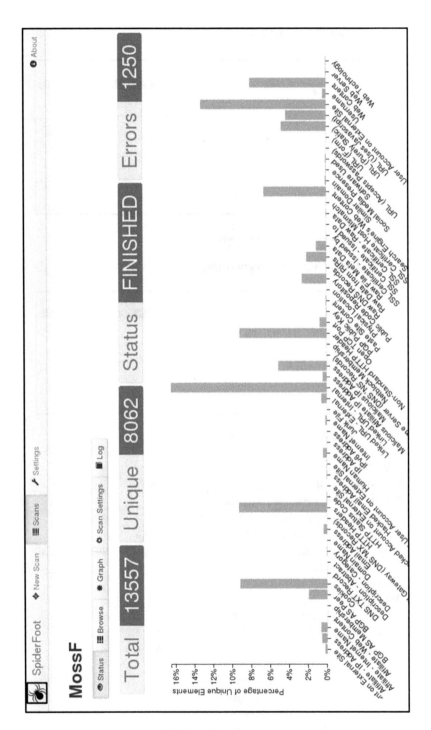

Figure 66 Spiderfoot mossfon.com OSINT search results

Click **Hacked Email Address**

Figure 67 Spiderfoot mossfon.com Hacked Emails module details

Click on **URL (Accepts Passwords)**

Figure 68 Spiderfoot mossfon.com USL (Accepts Passwords) module results

Module	Data/Source
Hacked Email Accounts	Support@Mossfon.com [Adobe]
	support@Mossfon.com [Last.fm]
	efonseca@Mossfon.com [LinkedIn]
	zollinger@Mossfon.com [Dropbox]
URL (Accepts Passwords)	https://mailgate.mossfoowa.mossfonn.com:8443/loginPage.imss
	owa.Mossfon.com
Other data	Accounts on external sites
	Hacked email account on External site
	Hacked User account on External site
	IPv6 address
	Malicious Affiliate IP address
	Malicious IP address
	PGP Public Key
	Open TCP Port
	Raw file metadata

SLL errors
Username
Web technology

Spiderfoot DNC.org OSINT Search

Start Spiderfoot, open a web browser and go to:
http://127.0.0.1:5001. Press the **New Scan** button. Enter Scan Name
= **dnc.** In the field called **Seed Target**, put in the domain URL
dnc.org. Use the default of **All.** Press the **Run Scan** button at the
bottom. During the scan or after completion, click **Browse.**

Click **User Account on External Site**

Figure 69 Spiderfoot DNC.org User Account on External Site search result

Check the **krolla@dnc.org** Adult Finder link in Data Element

Figure 70 Adult Finder profile for username Krolla from krolla@dnc.org

Click **Browse** to go back, then click **Hacked Email Addresses.**

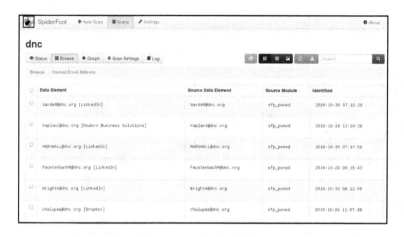

Figure 71 Spiderfoot DNC.org Hacked Email Addresses module search results

What have we learned? The DNC.org domain has been around for a while. Many staff over the years have set up accounts on external websites using their DNC email accounts. Some of those staffers appear lonely, looking for relationships outside their workplace, especially "special fellas."

Breaches happen, and some of the credentials have spilt out online for some of the Spiderfoot discovered external accounts using DNC email addresses. It is quite common for people to recycle or reuse passwords. An attacker could try and use previously breached credentials to get into the DNC, or use variants. A pattern could emerge if the same person is listed in several password breaches. Maybe their passwords use specific keywords or known information. For example, the victim uses spring, then spring-1, then spring-2, likely the user likes the word spring and when they change their password, keeps it easy and appends with a number..

Module	Data/Source
Hacked Email Accounts	gardem@dnc.org [LinkedIn]
	kaplanj@dnc.org [Modern Business Solutions]
	marshall@dnc.org [LinkedIn]
	paustenbachm@dnc.org [LinkedIn]
	wrighta@dnc.org [LinkedIn]
	Chalupaa@dnc.org [Dropbox]
User account	frankc@dnc.org [Adult Finder]
	krolla@dnc.org [Adult Finder]

on	marquez@dnc.org [Adult Finder]
external	parrishd@dnc.org [Adult Finder]
site	

Spiderfoot Kiesraad.nl OSINT Search

Start Spiderfoot, open a web browser and go to: **http://127.0.0.1:5001.** Press the **New Scan** button. Enter Scan Name = **Kiesraad.** In the field called **Seed Target**, put in the domain URL **kiesraad.nl.** Use the default of **All.** Press the **Run Scan** button at the bottom. During the scan or after completion, click **Browse.**

Click **Software Used**

Figure 72 Spiderfoot Kiesraad.nl Software Used module search result

Click **Browse,** then click **Vulnerability in Public Doman**

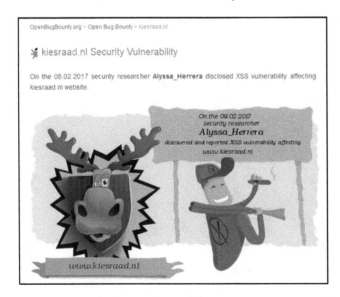

Alyssa_Herrera discovered a nice little cross site scripting vulnerability on the website on 2 February, 2017.

Module	Data/Source
Software used	Cannon, Altova Stylevision Enterprise Edition 2015 rel.4, Adobe Photoshop CS6 (Macintosh) Adobe Photoshop CS6 (Windows), Office 2007, Ricoh Aficio MP C4502, Xerox WorkCentre 5335, Xerox WorkCentre 5855, Xerox WorkCentre 7556
Vulnerabilit y in Public Doman	Open Bounty: https://www.openbugbounty.org/incidents/21205 5/ Cross Site Scripting on the Kiesraad.nl website February 2017
Other data	IPv6 address

Spiderfoot DonaldJTrump.com OSINT Search

Start Spiderfoot, open a web browser and go to: **http://127.0.0.1:5001.** Press the **New Scan** button. Enter Scan Name = **TheDon**. In the field called **Seed Target**, put in the domain URL **DonaldJTrump.com**. Use the default of **All**. Press the **Run Scan** button at the bottom. During the scan or after completion, click **Browse**.

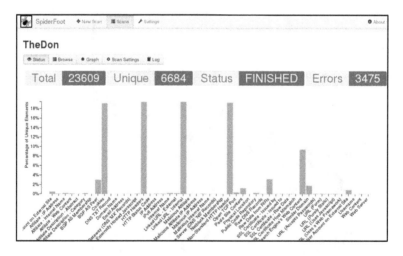

Figure 73 Spiderfoot DonaldJTrump.com OSINT search

Click the **Browse** button, then click **Malicious Affiliate**

Figure 74 Spiderfoot DonaldJTrump.com Malicious Affiliate module search result

Click **Browse,** then click **URL (Accepts Passwords)**

Figure 75 Spiderfoot DonaldJTrump.com URL (Accepts Passwords) module search result

Module	Data/Source
Malicious affiliate	Donaldjtrump.com.mail.protection.outlook.com PhishTank http://data.phishtank.com/data/online-valid.csv
URL (Accepts Passwords)	Email.donaldjtrump.com http://email. donaldjtrump.com http://email. donaldjtrump.com/# http://email. donaldjtrump.com /login

References

Spiderfoot. 2016. *SpiderFoot Documentation.* 20 September. http://www.spiderfoot.net/documentation/.

Tivārī, Gajendra. 1996. "Amana Prakāśana." In *Rañja līḍara ko bahuta hai*, by Gajendra Tivārī, 1. University of California.

Chapter 10

OSINT scanning Zen

INFORMATION IN THIS CHAPTER:

- Nmap and Zenmap overview
- Setting up customized script profiles
- Zenmap mossfon.com script scan
- Zenmap UKIP.org script scan
- Zenmap Geertwilders.nl script scan

CONTENTS

He that knows least commonly presumes most.

- Ub Narasinga Roa

10 Nmap and Zenmap

From Wikipedia "Nmap (Network Mapper) is a security scanner originally written by Gordon Lyon (also known by his pseudonym Fyodor Vaskovich)] used to discover hosts and services on a computer network, thus creating a "map" of the network. To accomplish its goal, Nmap sends specially crafted packets to the target host and then analyse the responses.

The software provides several features for probing computer networks, including host discovery and service and operating system detection. These features are extensible by scripts that provide more advanced service discovery, vulnerability detection, and other features. Nmap is also capable of adapting to network conditions including latency and congestion during a scan. Nmap is under development and refinement for its user community."

The power and usefulness of Nmap are its timing and scripts. Zenmap is the GUI of Nmap. What started as a network scanning tool has been expanded to a multi-purpose tool from scanning, reconnaissance & exploitation. The Nmap scripts can also be customized using the Lua programming language. If you are new to Nmap, I suggest using Zenmap, with Nmap command line or terminal. Everything you can do in the GUI you can do without a GUI. But, the GUI will help you learn and avoid a bunch of typos.

The main script categories are:
- ☑ auth(entication)
- ☑ default
- ☑ discovery
- ☑ external
- ☑ intrusive
- ☑ malware
- ☑ safe
- ☑ version
- ☑ vuln(erability)

Good Reconnaissance scripts to consider using:
- **Address-info** is default, safe: Extra information about IPv4&6 addresses
- **Asn-query** is default, external, safe: Maps IP addresses to AS autonomous systems.
- **Auth-owners** is default, safe: Tries to find the owner of a TCP port
- **Banner** is default, safe: connects to any open TCP port and tries to uess the service and version
- **http-apache-negotiation** is discovery, safe: Checks the target http server if the mod_negotiation setting is enabled.
- **http-date** is discovery, safe: Gets dates, http pipe and lots of SMB information
- **http-headers** is discovery, safe: Preforms a HEAD request for the root "/" folder of a web server
- **http-mobileversion-checker** is discover, safe: Checks if the

website has a mobile version
- **http-robots.txt** is discover, safe: checks if there are web pages an organization doesn't want indexed by a search engine
- **Shodan-api** is discovery, external, safe: it uses a Shodan API and queries information about the target.
- **Ssl-cert** is default, discover and safe: Checks the target's SSL certificate information.

Mossfon.com Robots.txt Scan

There are multiple methods of getting a robots.txt file. This file contains a note to search engines to please not index certain websites. Google respects robots.txt, but some other search engines do not. Robots is usually the first place I look for what the target wants to keep out of search engines.

Open ZenMap and type the **Mossfon.com** in Target box. Press the **Profile** button. Select **New Profile (Ctrl + P)**. Name it **robots.** Go to **scripts.** Pick the **http-robotx.txt.** Then click Save. Run the new profile by dropping down the Profile box and choosing **robots.**

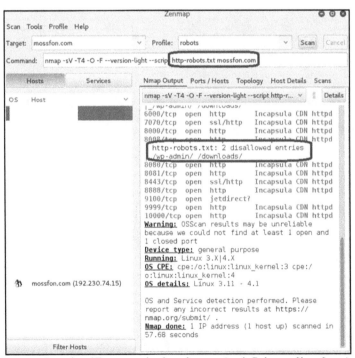

Figure 76 Screenshot of Zenmap results of mossfon.com using the Robots profile configuration

Test if the links exist. /downloads did not, but **/wp-admin** was a valid URL link.

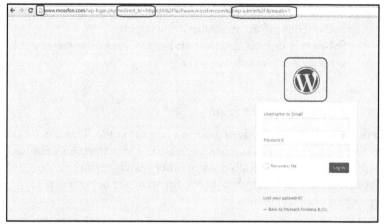

Figure 77 Screenshot test showing the URL for WordPress listed in Robots.txt was true

Open the **Host** details tab

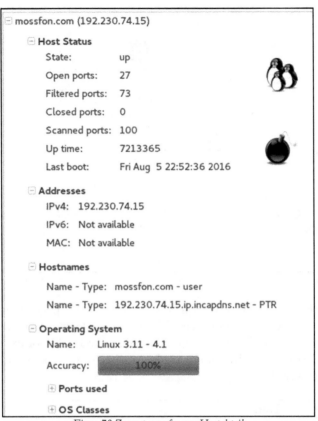

Figure 78 Zenmap mossfon.com Host details

Open the **Topology** tab, then click the **Fisheye** button.

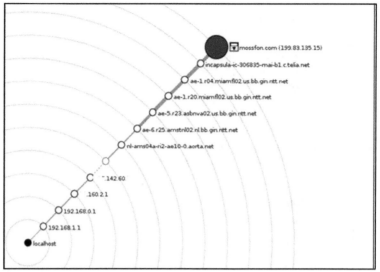

Figure 79 Zenmap mossfon.com Fisheye details

The link shows a Word Press administrator login page. It is over HTTP, unencrypted, not over HTTPS. This login offers no real security. Additionally, there is a forced redirect to HTTP for the admin page. Clearly, the URL shows inadequate security for a Word Press administrative login page.

Script	Data
http-	/downloads/
robots	/wp-admin/
Other	Word Press administrative login over HTTP

UKIP.org Nmap OSINT Scan

Open ZenMap and type the **UKIP.org** in Target box. Click the **Profile** button. Select **New Profile (Ctl + P)** and name it **OSINT**. Next go to **scripts** and select the **address-info, asn-query, banner, http-date, http-headers**, and the **http-robots.txt** scripts. Click **Save** button to save the profile settings. Run the new profile by dropping down the Profile box and choosing **OSINT.**

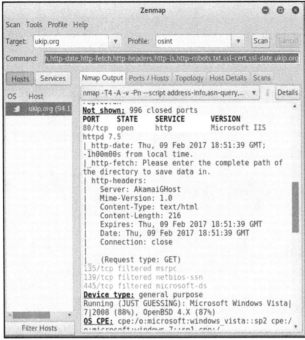

Figure 80 Screenshot of Zenmap results of UKIP.org using the OSINT profile configuration

UKIP.org appears to be running Microsoft IIS 7.5 over port 80 HTTP. Also, some no closed but filtered ports which are dangerous to have exposed on the internet. Posts 135, 139, and 445.

Module	Data/Source
Banner	Microsoft IIS 7.5 over port 80
	Port 135 Filtered
	Port 139 Filtered
	Port 445 Filtered
Other data	Services possibly exposed to the internet
	MSRPC
	Netbios-ssn
	Microsoft-ds directory services

Geertwilders.nl Nmap OSINT Scan

Open ZenMap and type the **geertwilders.nl** in Target box. Go to **Profile** drop down box and select **OSINT**. Press **Scan.** Wait for the scan to run and results will populate. The script **http-robots.txt** reported 18 URLs not to index by search engines. Out of the 18, one URL yielded a result. An administrative login, which was unencrypted on port 80 HTTP at **http://geertwilders.nl/administrator/**

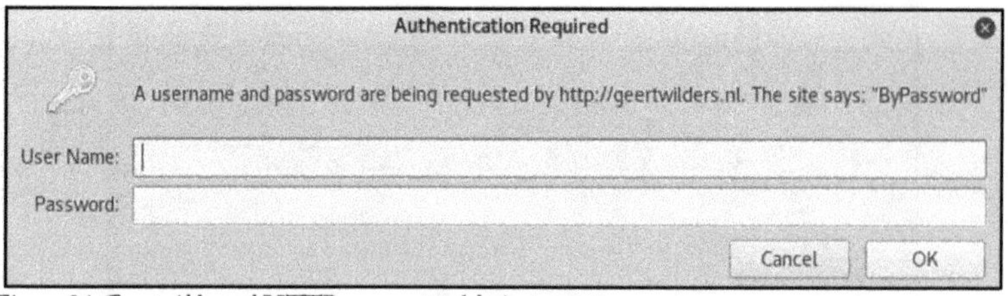

Figure 81 Geertwilders.nl HTTP unencrypted login prompt

Figure 82 Geertwilders.nl authentication failure error page showing Apache webserver

The script **banner** reported multiple ports and services. Some filtered Microsoft ports at 135, 139 and RPC ports 111 TCP and UDP, 877 UDP and 888 TCP.

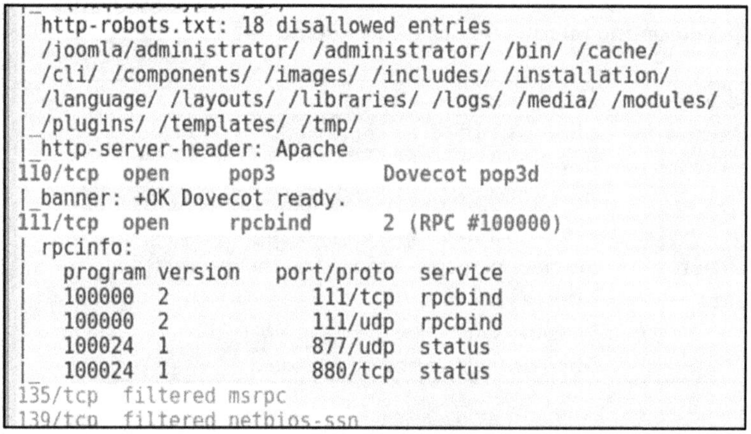

Figure 83 Geertwilders.nl Zenmap results showing open and filtered ports

To view more detail sof what services are running actively on what ports. Press the **Ports** tab.

	Port	Protocol	State	Service	Version
✓	21	tcp	open	ftp	Pure-FTPd
✓	22	tcp	open	ssh	OpenSSH 4.3 (protocol 1.99)
✓	25	tcp	open	smtp	Sendmail 8.13.8/8.13.8
✓	80	tcp	open	http	Apache httpd
✓	110	tcp	open	pop3	Dovecot pop3d
✓	111	tcp	open	rpcbind	2 (RPC #100000)
✗	135	tcp	filtered	msrpc	
✗	139	tcp	filtered	netbios-ssn	
✓	143	tcp	open	imap	Dovecot imapd
✓	443	tcp	open	ssl	Apache httpd (SSL-only mode)
✗	445	tcp	filtered	microsoft-ds	
✓	465	tcp	open	smtps	
✓	587	tcp	open	smtp	Sendmail 8.13.8/8.13.8
✓	880	tcp	open	status	1 (RPC #100024)
✓	3306	tcp	open	mysql	MySQL 5.0.95
✓	5666	tcp	open	tcpwrapped	
✓	8080	tcp	open	http	Apache httpd

Figure 84 Geertwilders.nl Zenmap Host detail results

Some of the ports are considered risky to have open or filtered.

Module	Data/Source
Banner	Apache web server
	Ports open: 21, 22, 25, 80, 110, 111, 143, 443,
	465, 587, 880, 3306, 5666, 8080
	Ports filtered: 135, 139, 445
Other data	Services possibly exposed to the internet
	MSRPC
	Netbios-ssn
	Microsoft-ds directory services
	MySQL

Geertwilders.nl & PVV.nl Vulnerability Review

Lots of open or filtered, partially exposed ports viewable from the internet. Older, vulnerable web server versions, a series of ports for RPC and Microsoft directory services which are known to have major security issues happily open or giving mixed messages. I would be surprised if the organization's website hasn't been compromised. It might be actively compromised now, with all those ports and visible weak configuration. The PVV is more than capable of hiring local talent and businesses to help secure it's website. The party has been accused of not paying staff correctly in the past, this could be a visible sign of it.

One of the ports partially exposed to the internet carries some major risks. From the Malware Tops forum:

"Once an attacker discovers an active port 139 on a device, he can run NBSTAT to begin the very important first step of an attack—foot printing. With the NBSTAT command, he can obtain some or all of the following information:

- Computer name
- Contents of the remote name cache, including IP addresses
- A list of local NetBIOS names
- A list of names resolved by broadcast or via WINS
- Contents of the session table with the destination IP addresses"

References

NMap. n.d. *Home page.* Accessed May 1, 2016. Grabbing banners and naming services.

Roa, Ub Narasinga. 1994. "A Handbook of Kannada Proverbs, with English Equivalents." In *A Handbook of Kannada Proverbs, with English Equivalents*, by Ub Narasinga Roa, 5. New Delhi: Asian Educational Series.

Wikipedia. 2016. *Nmap.* April 04. 2016 https://en.wikipedia.org/wiki/Nmap.

API data transformations

Although our intellect always longs for clarity and certainty, our nature often finds uncertainty fascinating.
- Carl von Clausewitz

11 Maltego

Maltego is a graphical OSINT tool which uses transforms to connect data to entities using security and search engine databases and API queries. For the lab use the free, community edition. It is limited to 12 transforms. Many intelligence teams use Maltego commercial versions with Case File and run internal transform servers. In previous, professional positions. My team and I had fun writing custom transforms and linking to our data sources.

Maltego loves memory so run it in a nice sized machine. RAM, CPU,

CPU processors. Install the free transforms; most are relevant to OSINT. The free IMDB movies transform isn't required for OSINT. There is a learning curve to the product, try not to get too frustrated. Maltego Kali uses a captcha when logging in.

Maltego Mossack Fonseca Company Stalker

We will use Maltego to take a light look at Mossfon.com, the primary domain of Mossack Fonseca. While you are learning Maltego, it's important to note there is a Panama Papers transform and an extensive write up by the Maltego team on how to find relationships related to the leaked papers. The Maltego setting, Company Stalker will look at any information which it believes is related to the domain. We are using it a passive reconnaissance manner. The Mossack Fonseca research was accomplished using Maltego version 3 CE. Your Maltego might look slightly different.

Open and Log into Maltego. Chose the **Company Stalker** option. Type: **Mossfon.com**. Allow Maltego to run, which might take a while. You might be asked a few times about running some transforms, be careful to use only **non-intrusive transformations.** Maltego will bring up a whole bunch of email addresses and websites on the website.

Highlight the email address **zollinger@Mossfon.com**. Run the Machine called **@haveibeenpwned** if it does not run automatically.

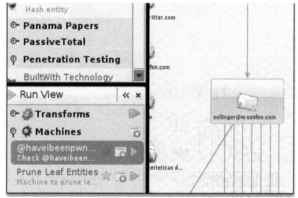

Figure 85 Maltego mossfon.com @haveibeenpwned transform screenshot

The transform will show the email is listed in a database called **@haveibeenpwned**. Zoom in on the results.

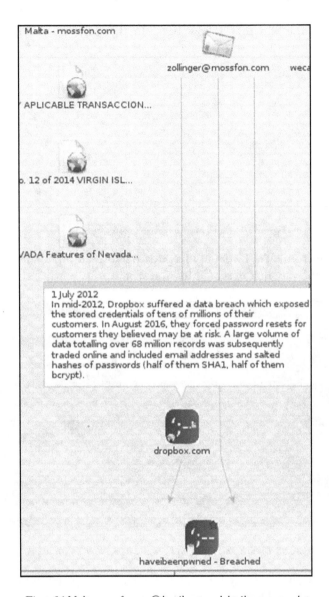

Malta - mossfon.com

zollinger@mossfon.com   weca

' APLICABLE TRANSACCION...

b. 12 of 2014 VIRGIN ISL...

/ADA Features of Nevada...

> 1 July 2012
> In mid-2012, Dropbox suffered a data breach which exposed
> the stored credentials of tens of millions of their
> customers. In August 2016, they forced password resets for
> customers they believed may be at risk. A large volume of
> data totalling over 68 million records was subsequently
> traded online and included email addresses and salted
> hashes of passwords (half of them SHA1, half of them
> bcrypt).

dropbox.com

haveibeenpwned - Breached

Figure 86 Maltego mossfon.com @haveibeenpwned detail zoom screenshot

Due to a Dropbox breach in 2012. The email credentials were leaked. In the Pallet section, double click the **Twit entity.** Go to the **Properties** tab. Change the Username to **@Mossfon** for Twitter. Right click the **Twitter/Twit entity.** Run the available **Twitter transforms.** You might have to sign into Twitter, if so create a quick fake account. Sign-in can take forever and fail. Rick click the **Twit entity.** Run transforms: **To Twitter Followers** and **To Twitter Friends**. Maltego will return who follows @Mossfon's Twitter account and who they follow back. In this case, it's mainly news agencies.

Figure 87 Maltego Twitter transforms results for mossfon.com

Run transform: **To Tweets [That this person wrote].** You can now pull up the very first tweet @Mossfon sent.

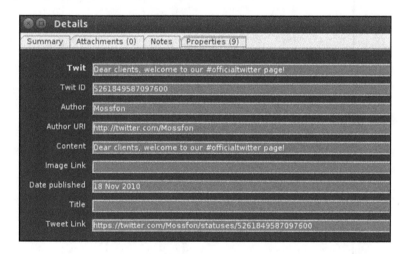

Figure 88 The first Tweet Mossack Fonseca sent from their Twitter account

By the way, not too wise for a law firm which sets up very confidential client packages. Don't ask or promote clients follow you. Circled are possible customers:

Figure 89 Twitter followers screenshot showing possible clients of Mossack Fonseca

Change or look at the Maltego **Entity List**. Scroll down to web sites and click into the details of **Crypt.Mossfon.com.**

Figure 90 Maltego Entity detail list for Mossack Fonseca

Double click and go into the **properties**. The Crypt, an archive server is running an outdated version of Microsoft IIS 7.5.

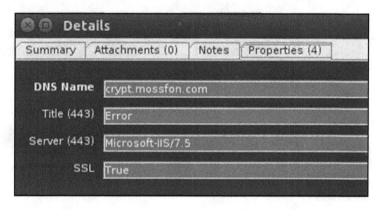

Figure 91 Maltego details of Cyrpt.mossfon.com running an IIS 7.5 webserver

Some relevant information about the target was found.

Transform/Machine	Entity	Data
Company Stalker	Mossfon.com	Staff email accounts Zollinger@Mossfon.com Additional email accounts which belong to staff outside Mossfon.com
@haveibeenpwned.	Zollinger@Mossfon.com	Dropbox breach 2012
Company Stalker/Banner grabbing of subdomain	Mossfon.com	Uses Neustar Aggregate Knowledge (DMP) identity management PHP Framework present Unknown assets
Company Stalker/Banner grabbing of subdomain	Mossfon.com	Mfblog.Mossfon.com Apps.mpssfon.com Helpdesk.Mossfon.com
To Tweets [That this person wrote]	@Mossfon	Possible clients following the target
Company Stalker/Banner grabbing of subdomain	Crypt.Mossfon.com	Microsoft IIS 7.5 SSL Might have a certificate issue causing the Error

Maltego DNC.org Domain Analysis

Open and Log into Maltego. Chose the **Domain Analysis** option. Fill in **DNC.org.** Click Next. In the New Graph tab, the **DNC.org** will show as a sphere icon and will be populated with some data. Highlight the **DNC.org** icon. Click the **Run** view to expand. Scroll down and use the transform **To Email Address [PGP]**

The New Graph area will populate with all the known public PGP keys associated with the DNC.org domain and a PGP key in a PGP Key Server.

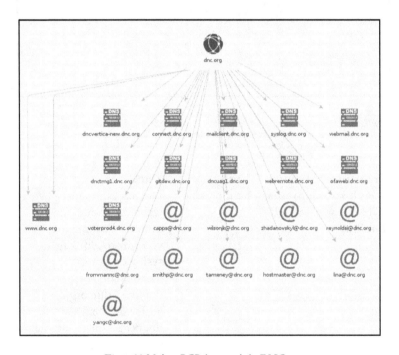

Figure 92 Maltego PGP keys result for DNC.org

Highlight **DNC.org.** Run the transform **[Threat Miner] Domain to APT Nodes].** This transform retunes and IP address or addresses of malware that connects to the domain. A document from Dell Secureworks will populate, called **Threat Grup-4124 Targets Hillary Clinton Presidential Campaign – Dell Secureworks.pdf**

Highlight **DNC.org.** Run the transform **[ThreatCrowdEnrichDomain].** The results show an IP address which was observed sending malware to the DNC.org. IP address 104.239.151.78.

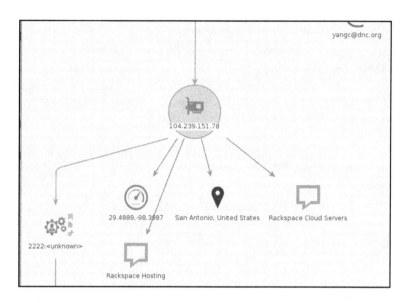

yangc@dnc.org

104.239.151.78

29.4889,-98.3987   San Antonio, United States   Rackspace Cloud Servers

2222:<unknown>

Rackspace Hosting

Figure 93 Maltego ThreatCrowdEnrichDomain zoom screenshot showing 104.239.151.78 as a malware sending IP address to the DNC.org

Transform/Machine	Entity	Data
Search sub-domains (DNSDumpster, SP Toolkit)	Subdomains	Dncuag1.dnc.org, webremote.dnc.org, ofaweb.dnc.org, voterprod4.dnc.org, syslog.dnc.org, webmail.dnc.org, dnctmg1.dnc.org, gitdev.dnc.org, dncvertica-new.dnc.org, www.dnc.org
To Email Address [PGP]	PGP Keys	capps@dnc.com, wilsonjk@dnc.org, zhadnovskyl@dnc.org, reynoldsi@dnc.org, frommannc@dnc.org, smithp@dnc.org, tameney@dnc.org, hostmaster@dnc.org, lina@dnc.org, yangc@dnc.com
[Threat Miner] Domain to APT Nodes	Threat intelligence report	Threat Group-4124 Targets Hillary Clinton Presidential Campaign –

[Threat Miner] Domain to APT Nodes]	Domains	Dell Secureworks.pdf 104.239.151.78 Possible source of malware at one time

The PGP keys listed indicates the DNC had and have the ability to encrypt emails, important emails. Important leaked emails; such as, donor information, strategy and other important and confidential information. PGP can encrypt and can also be used to decrypt emails and attachments which should be in the public record by law. The DNC email leak did not contain any PGP emails. The DNC was a regular email leak, all unencrypted emails. Email protocols by default are unencrypted. If emails are not encrypted, they travel over the Internet in clear text, where any ISP or spy agency with the right connections can see all the emails anyway. Not a leak in my opinion.

DNC Vulnerability Review

A VPN is supposed to be setup primarily to encrypt traffic and create a private, encrypted, secure tunnel. The DNC VPN, no encryption or authentication was turned on. When staff use a VPN, they typically believe the connection is secure. When people think communications are secure, they tend to have confidential conversations. The Shodan screenshot was taken after the breach, after the suspicions of foreign spy agencies taking part in the breach. If I found the VPN with such weak settings. How many others found it as well?

Riskiest vulnerabilities from a hacker perspective:

Data Type	Data	Data Source
Compromised accounts on external web sites	Credential recycling could be in use allowing easier entry	Spiderfoot
PGP Keys		Spiderfoot/Maltego
Leaked personally identifiable information	Donor, staff, strategy and confidential communications information leaked	WikiLeaks
Webserver	Nginx 1.0 version	Spiderfoot
Insecure VPN configuration	No encryption, or authentication enabled	Shodan
External accounts	Adult Finder and other dating websites linked to	Spiderfoot

possibly tied to staff	official DNS email accounts could be used for social engineering/phishing.

Many of the DNC servers showed up in Spiderfoot running older versions of Linux. Most of discoveries were information great for social engineering. Some paste dumps which could be promising. The documents in WikiLeaks, awesome for social engineering. I didn't observe any news stories where the DNC was giving credit monitoring to people whose personal data was leaked. Donor information with money amounts, personally identifiable information and tax payer identification numbers should not have been emailed in an insecure manner. However, the USA has a culture of unnecessary, insecure usage of their tax payer identification number. There is also no real privacy law in the USA, other than for medical data. This is shocking after living in Europe.

The DNC has had secure email capabilities. Ten PGP keys. PGP can allow both secure email and the ability for any required government transparency. No need for staffers to run to secure communications which cannot be shared with the US government where required. Some communications are required to be shared to keep parties supposedly more honest. Funny how the DNC had PGP keys but Mrs. Clinton didn't use any.

As if it required special skills to leak unencrypted emails. A convenient excuse such as Advanced Persistent Threat to try and explain away poor IT security or blame spooky spies. All the DNC emails leaked were unencrypted, not requiring an advanced attack, more like a sniffer.

Maltego DonaldJTrump.com Company Stalker

Open and Log into Maltego. Chose the **Company Stalker** option. Type: **DonaldJTrump.com**. Let Maltego run, which might take a while. You might be asked to discard a catch all email address, clock the Proceed With button and discard the **now@donaldjtrump.com email**.

Figure 94 Maltego false positive tuning, excluding and email address

If asked, allow the **emailToMySpaceAccount** to run by accepting the disclaimer and remembering the settings.

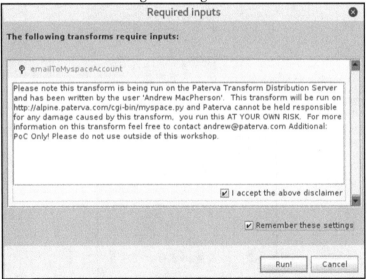

Figure 95 Maltego transform warning message

The result will be "huge". So big, you will have to zoom out to a dot view.

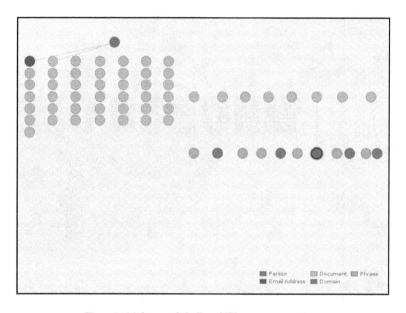

Figure 96 Maletgo result for DonaldJTrump.com zoomed out

Zoom into the bottom right section and notice software versions and a printer.

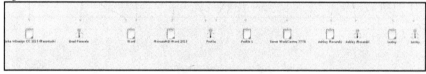

Figure 97 Maltego assets result from DonalJTrump.com document metadata

Zoom into the printer.

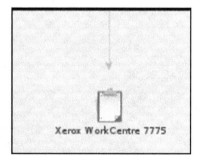

Figure 98 Xerox WorkCentre 7775 Printer obtained from Maltego metadata parser

The zoom in shows software and printers in use picked up from metadata and other analysis with transforms. One sticks out, a Xerox WorkCenter 7775 printer. Also, Adobe InDesign CC 2015 Macintosh,

Microsoft Word 2013, some names such as Brad Parscale, Lesley and Ashly Mocarski.

Transform/Machine	Entity	Data
Company Stalker	Applications in use	Adobe InDesign CC 2015 (Macintosh) Microsoft Word 2013
Company Stalker	Real names	Brad Parscale Lesley Ashly Mocarski
Company Stalker	Printer	Xerox WorkCenter 7775

Trump Vulnerability Review

Trump Hotel, Toronto's old, vulnerable and highly insecure FTP server FileZilla was not expected. Also, not expected to find it in 4 minutes, after Trump Hotels New York had been fined the same month for poor IT security leading to a customer breach.

Go to **Exploit-db.com.** Search **Filezilla.** Prove you are not a robot if asked. Get all the available exploits and proof of concept (PoC) code available. You can also download the vulnerable software to test yourself in a lab and hack it.

Date ▾	D	A	V	Title	Platform	Author
2016-05-11	⬇	🗔	⊚	FileZilla FTP Client 3.17.0.0 - Unquoted Path Privilege Escalation	Windows	Cyril Valli...
2015-08-07	⬇	🗔	✔	FileZilla Client 2.2.x - Buffer Overflow (SEH)	Windows	ly0n
2015-06-15	⬇	🗔	✔	FileZilla 3.11.0.2 SFTP Module - Denial of Service	Windows	3unnym00n
2006-12-11	⬇	🗔	✔	FileZilla FTP Server 0.9.21 - (LIST/NLST) Denial of Service	Windows	shinnai
2006-12-09	⬇	🗔	✔	FileZilla FTP Server 0.9.20b/0.9.21 - (STOR) Denial of Service	Windows	rgod
2005-11-21	⬇	🗔	✔	FileZilla Server Terminal 0.9.4d - Buffer Overflow (PoC)	Windows	Inge Henriksen
2005-09-02	⬇	-	✔	FileZilla 2.2.15 - FTP Client Hard-Coded Cipher Key	Windows	m123303@ric...

Figure 99 Exploit-db.com Filezilla exploits available

The version 0.936 running in Toronto is vulnerable to many of the exploits listed in the database. Buffer overflows, denial of service and hard coded credentials are listed in the exploit database. At time of writing, the current version of FileZilla is 3.24.0. Last tested, February 2017 and the same old, vulnerable version of FileZilla at Trump Hotel Toronto.

Riskiest vulnerabilities from a hacker perspective:

Data Type	Data	Data Source
Applications in use	Adobe InDesign 2015 MS Word 2013	Maltego
Printer	Xerox WorkCentre 7775	Maltego
Personally identifiable information	Three staff member's names	WikiLeaks
Shell Companies	Several companies and holdings which are tied to Trump Towers, NYC and other properties	ICIJ Database
Insecure FTP software	FileZilla 0.936	Shodan/telnet

References

Offensive Security. (2016, April 02). *Offensive Security's Exploit Database Archive*. Retrieved from Exploit Database: https://www.exploit-db.com/

Rapid 7. (2016, April 02). *Rapid 7 Vulnerability & Exploit Database*. Retrieved from Rapid 7: https://www.rapid7.com/db/

Fear the metadata

INFORMATION IN THIS CHAPTER:

- FOCA overview
- Setting up FOCA for scanning metadata only
- FOCA metadata analysis of GOP.com
- FOCA metadata analysis of Kiesraad.nl
- Case Study: FOCA and the NRC

Yet the deepest truths are best read between the lines, and, for the most part, refuse to be written.

- Amos Bronson Alcott

12 FOCA

FOCA is a Windows based, multi-purpose penetration testing tool. It has a nice GUI, easy to use and fast. It's great for all around general penetration testing. However, I use it mainly to quickly download and analyze metadata from documents.

Configure FOCA for Safe Use

This project focuses on OSINT, not exploitative penetration testing.

The tool can be used for exploitative testing, so be careful. Configure FOCA to download and use for metadata analysis only.

Open FOCA.exe. Go to **Options.** Open the **Exploiting** tab. Uncheck everything in **SQLi**. Open the **LFI/RFI** tab. Uncheck everything in LFI/RFI. Open **Common enforcement errors** tab. Uncheck everything in Common enforcement errors. Open **Common enforcement errors.** Open **Directorie**s tab. Uncheck **Search for multiple choices.** Uncheck **Search for CVE-2012-1823.** Uncheck **Search automatically for IIS shortname vulnerability.** Press the **Save** button

GOP.com FOCA Metadata Scan

Open FOCA.exe. Go to **Project.** Select **New Project.** Type **GOP** in the Project name. Type **gop.com** in the Domain website Pick a location to save the documents. Press the **Create** button. Highlight **Metadata** in the left project view

Figure 100 FOCA Metadata section

Press the **Search All** button

Figure 101 FOCA Document scan options detail

FOCA will now begin to search both Google and Bing with Dorks to

find documents which are posted publicly, unencrypted. As FOCA scans search engines, the Documents field will populate. Once FOCA is finished, right click a document. Select **Download** or **Download All**. FOCA downloads at a very passive pace. Once all or most of the documents are downloaded, right click again and pick **Extract Metadata.**

Once complete, right click again and select **Analyze Metadata.** The Project view will begin to populate with information parsed from the metadata.

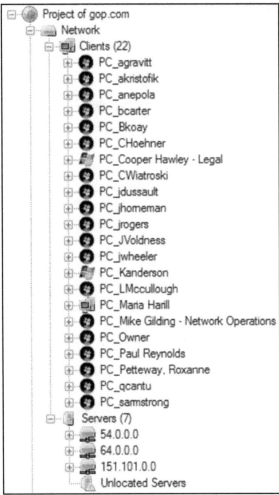

Figure 102 FOCA metadata analysis results for network and clients from the GOP.com website

Twenty-two computers, three netblock ranges, operating systems and software in use, real names, important computers. A good deal of information is returned from the metadata. Expand the **Metadata** folder. Highlight **Software** to show the software in use.

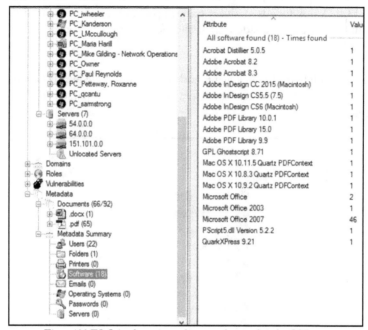

Figure 103 FOCA software in use from metadata analysis for GOP.com

Highlight **PC_Mike Gilding – Network Operations**

Attribute	Value
Information	
Name	PC_Mike Gilding - Network Operations
Operating System	Windows Vista
Users	
Mike Gilding - Network Operations	
Software	
Microsoft Office 2007	
Documents used to infer this computer	
https://cdn.gop.com/docs/Rules-of-the-Republican-Party.pdf	

Figure 104 FOCA result for PC_Mike Gilding - Network Operations from metadata GOP.com

Module	Data/Source
Network	Microsoft Vista
Operations	Microsoft Office 2
computer	Real name possible: Mike Gilding
	PC Name
Computer	PC_agravtt, PC_akristofik, PC_anepola, PC_bcarter,

128

names	PC_Bkoay, PC_CHoehner, PC_Cooper Hawley – Legal, PC_CWaitroski, PC_idussault, PC_jhomeman, PC_jrogers, PCJVoldness, PC_jwheeler, PC_Kanderson, PC_LMccullough, PC_Maria HAril, PC_Mike Gilding – Network Operations, PC_Owner, PC_Paul Reynolds, PC_Petteway, Roxanne, PC_qcantu, PC_samstrong
Netblocks	54.0.0.0
	64.0.0.0
	151.101.0.0

GOP Vulnerability Review

Network operations and lawyer computers were nice discoveries. Especially the network operations computer. Social engineering information. After watching a Sam Bowne presentation, he stated a study which calculated spear phishing attacks are successful about 20% of the time. I love math and statistics in the case; the odds are in the attacker's favour. Looking over the documents, many recently created documents were from computers running old, outdated and unsupported Microsoft Office versions. I like printers, using them extensively in the past to get into networks and grab sensitive documents. Printer/scanner/copier combo office devices have hard drives installed, which commonly keep a record of everything scanned. Particularly helpful for a human resources department target. Printers are not tested for security as extensively as some other software and firmware. Most now run a web server, many are exposed to the internet and are insecurely setup with default credentials. These are extra yummy. The printer model from Xerox had a security warning when I went to download the user manual..

Xerox Security Message: Reminder to Set Firmware Password on Networked Devices

Security is a top priority for Xerox. Anything connected to the network – whether a fax machine, copier, printer, scanner, or PC – is vulnerable to outside attacks. It's a topic we discuss often on the security website, and we continue to share with our customers the importance of securing safely all of their devices.

Specific to the remote firmware threats that have been highlighted by researchers, the majority of Xerox products have user-enabled countermeasures to diminish this type of threat, including:
- Simple password settings
- System administrator-settable enablement of software upgrade
- Requirement that firmware updates must be digitally signed from Xerox to verify authenticity.

For the most recent security updates please continue to visit this site. If you have questions on how to best lock down your Xerox device, contact your sales rep, submit a request online at http://www.xerox.com/perl-bin/formeng.pl?form=product_security_information_request_7285, or call 1-800-821-2797 (U.S. only).

Xerox offers the following direction in regards to the recent National Cybersecurity and Communications Integration Center Bulletin 1-0012-NCCIC-130020120223:

Figure 105 Xerox security warning to harden and secure printers

I guess I'm not the only one which is curious about printers ☺

Kiesraad.nl Software Vulnerability and Metadata Hunt

In late January 2017, I found this intriguing post title on a sub-Reddit called Netsec. The title, "How to hack the upcoming Dutch elections – and how hackers could have hacked all Dutch elections since 2009" by Sijmen Ruwhof, a Dutch researcher/hacker. His blog post starts by presenting the ongoing investigation into possible Russian hacking into the DNC and the fears of election manipulation throughout Europe. Due to the ease of hacking electronic voting machines, the Dutch parliament outlawed them in 2009. However, software to tabulate the votes is allowed in a transparent manner, independently audited.

I thought to myself, wait a minute, I live in the Netherlands. The country as a whole is technologically advanced, early adopters of IPv6, have departments for future planning, everyone has access to high-speed internet. The voting board Kiesraad couldn't possibly be using critically vulnerable software to tabulate votes for an election. Sad hacker facepalm :0

Sijmen goes through the election tabulation software's instructional videos. It's called OSV. These videos are freely available on both the election board's website, Keisraad.nl and Youtube.com. Due to the E-voting law, section P2, instructions for use and documentation, along with source code and independent audit reports must be freely available on the Kiesraad.nl website. Though, that does not mean the

130

election board is required to show the level of detail the instructor did, which allowed discovery of critical weaknesses. These weaknesses, for the most part, had existed since the software was built, in 2009.

In the initial video Sijmen reviews. The instructor open's her desktop, shows network drives, reveals the tabulation software requires a local web server with simple, unencrypted authentication. The security capability involving hashing is highly flawed and create additional security issues and neuter secure hashing altogether. Sijmen goes into great detail, in English on his blog. Over 25 exploitable low to critical level vulnerabilities.

I decided to look a little further to see what else I could find. I am not fluent in Dutch. I am still learning the language, but Google has this wonderful tool called Google Translate which works most of the time. I looked through the Dutch version of the Kiesraad.nl website as it had the most information, understandably. I discovered a few more items of interest.

Keisraad.nl are required by Netherlands law to post the OSV software source code, independent audit report and technical documentation along with basic usage. Most of the requirements were met, but the technical documentation. They had instead posted an older version 1.4.3 posted on the website instead of the reviewed version is 2.17.2 in use.

The independent audit review, dated 19 February 2016, focuses on the tabulation calculation functions of the OSV software. The report does not focus on security but mentions some major security vulnerabilities. Page 7 of the report had a very interesting passage. The testing firm had brought up security issues in previous reports. Instead of remediating the security concerns, the election board believed the risk of voting manipulation was too low to consider important. The board, an appointed non-technical body, decided not to pay attention to the professional advice of the test and audit company. The

First Dutch, then a Google English translation:

- *Authenticiteit aangeleverde gegevens (eis 11, zie 4.11):* OSV is niet strikt in het afdwingen van de controle op authenticiteit van aangeleverde gegevens. Dit is begrijpelijk vanuit het perspectief van gebruiksvriendelijkheid van de software, maar vanuit een beveiligingsperspectief is dit niet minder wenselijk. **Volgens de Kiesraad zijn de organisatorische omstandigheden in die situaties zodanig dat de kans**

buitengewoon klein wordt geacht op optreden van het risico op misbruik.

- *Authenticity supplied data* (requirement 11, see 4.11): OSV is not strict in enforcing control authenticity of information provided. This is understandable from the perspective of usability of the software, but this is less desirable from a security perspective.

  According to the Electoral Council are the organizational conditions in those situations so that the probability is considered extremely small in occurrence of the risk of abuse.

Page 26 of the report details all the required software OSV needs to run correctly on a computer. This is helpful to attackers, since exploits can be found, bought or created:

- ☑ Eclipse Java EE IDE for Web Developers, Version: Indigo Service Release 1
- ☑ Altova StyleVision, version 2015 rel. 4
- ☑ JBoss Application Server, JBoss-4.2.3.GA
- ☑ Apache FOP 1.1, avalon-framework-4.2.0.jar, batik 1.7, Xalan-J 2.7.0, Xerces 2.7.1
- ☑ Apache Derby (version 10.11.1.1.) embedded database
- ☑ Apache POI 3.1
- ☑ XOM 1.1 XML object model

The newest instruction video posted in 2016 shows even more information which could be misused to gain access to tabulation systems and manipulate an election.

- ☑ More network drives
- ☑ More internal IP information
- ☑ Chrome browser with favorites
- ☑ Gmail used in the background, open
- ☑ A network drive with photos of swimming events

The 2016 Kiesraad OSV instructional videos indicated a high probability a tabulation computer was probably used for everyday office usage as well. I ran a FOCA scan on Kiesraad.nl to check if metadata would yield anything of value. FOCA discovered a computer which is used for the election tabulation software. It had been used to create a document which was posted online in 2015. FOCA couldn't get the computer name.

Attribute	Value
Information	
Name	PC_Unknown0
Software	
Apache FOP Version 0.95	
Altova StyleVision Enterprise Edition 2014 sp1 (http://www.altova.com)	
Documents used to infer this computer	
https://www.kiesraad.nl/binaries/kiesraad/documenten/publicaties/2015/02/16/overzicht-definitieve-kandi...	

Figure 106 FOCA metadata analysis showing which computer runs voting tabulation software deduced by the software installed

FOCA was also able to retrieve real names, computer names, including the Central Voting Bureau's cluster. All from the metadata of posted documents.

```
Network
    Clients (17)
        PC_Akse
        PC_BakkerM
        PC_Centraal Stembureau's (cluster)
        PC_chatrerp
        PC_evertse
        PC_Formzet Zoetermeer
        PC_Gonzalez
        PC_Hormann, Heleen
        PC_marjoleinwalsmit
        PC_Ministerie van Binnenlandse Zaken en Koninkrijksrelaties
        PC_Nehmelman, R. (Remco)
        PC_Océ-Technologies B.V.
        PC_Ruud Heemskerk
        PC_Unknown0
        PC_VoogdE
        PC_Walsmit
        PC_WoudeJK
```

Figure 107 FOCA metadata analysis Network details for Keisraad.nl

It is generally not a great idea to have a very critical computer used for the election tabulation of an entire country for every day, regular office use. Gmail, personal favourites, etc.… If I were a naughty attacker I could setup a watering hole attack on those favourite websites, social engineering with a swimming pictures or hook the browser via the Gmail account. So many evil cat things went through my head.

One of my favourite techniques to get control of a target computer or inside a target network is through web browser exploitation. Via JavaScript, an attacker can hook a web browser and leverage the victim's system to penetrate further. The victim machine, used as a bot or zombie. Network scans can be launched from the browser, credentials stolen from open browser tabs or a web camera turned on and took video or recording sound. Attackers have previously used watering hole attacks against high-value targets and journalists. Once regularly visited websites are known, an attacker can either exploit and place malicious JavaScript on it, or use malicious advertising and embed the hook there. There are many ways to exploit browsers as a penetration tester or an attacker.

After downloading the source code and opening in Notepad ++. The code shows J2SE/1.5 which is an old, outdated, vulnerable version of Java 5. There are exploits available for this old version.

```
org.eclipse.jdt.internal.debug.ui.launcher.StandardVMType/J2SE-1.5"/>
```

Figure 108 Section of source code for Dutch election vote tabulation software showing J2SE 1.5 required

Riskiest vulnerabilities from a hacker perspective:

Data Type	Data	Data Source
Existing authentication vulnerabilities	OSV software test and audit report	Keisraad.nl
Web site vulnerability	Cross site scripting vulnerability reported	Spiderfoot
Insecure VPN configuration	No encryption, or authentication enabled	Shodan
Internal IP, network and general usage	Information which could be used for social engineering/phishing.	YouTube, Keisraad.nl, FOCA

The story had a happy ending. Because of Sijmen's efforts and working with journalists on television. Parliament in the Netherlands was called to session and voted against using the vulnerable software. All 2017 notes will be hand counted instead. A great example of the power of hackers and OSINT. I love happy hacker endings.

After watching my first FOCA presentation at DefCon. I have used it to check out various organisations over the years. One of these is the Nuclear Regulatory Agency (NRC). The NRC has been compromised a few times over the years. Lots of phishing.

In 2013 I showed a presentation in London at the Cyber Senate ICS Security Europe conference called Confessions of an OT/IT Hacker. In the presentation, I showed some attack techniques used with case studies. One of the cases was the NRC. It had recently been compromised via phishing. I studied the attack and showed how the list of email addresses and names used in the attack could have been retrieved from metadata. A quick scan with FOCA showed 240 user names, 298 internal folder locations, 62 printers with IP addresses, 15 different emails and more. A treasure trove to start social engineering.

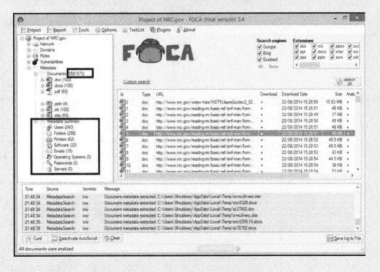

Figure 109 FOCA NRC.gov documents and metadata scan

It is very important to clean or strip as much metadata as possible from documents when posting online. Something which can be easily overlooked because of the manual cleaning process. Big organisations can purchase services which can strip metadata automatically. Sadly, document metadata isn't usually high on the risk register.

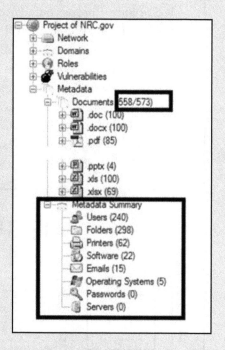

Figure 110 FOCA NRC.gov Metadata Summary details

References

Ruwhof, S. (2017, January 28). *How to Hack the Upcoming Dutch Elections*. Retrieved from Web Blog: https://sijmen.ruwhof.net/weblog/1166-how-to-hack-the-upcoming-dutch-elections

Where was that figure again?

What page was that again?

Who wrote this?

ABOUT THE AUTHOR

Chris Kubecka, Security Researcher and CEO of HypaSec. HypaSec offers expert advice, incident response management, lecturing, training in IT and ICS security, penetration testing, privacy and vulnerability scanning and writing services in security. HypaSec also build hands-on penetration and intelligence courses, such as a hands-on version of the GIAC GPEN. Formerly, she setup several security groups for Saudi Aramco's affiliates after the Shamon 1 attacks and held positions as Group Leader for Aramco Overseas, Netherlands. Implementing and leading the Security Operations Centre, Network Operation Centre and Joint International Intelligence Group & the EU/UK Privacy Group for Aramco Overseas Company. With >20 years of professional experience in the field, her career includes the US Air Force, Space Command, private and public sector.

A conference presenter at Black Hat, OWASP, Security BSides, CCC Chaos Computer Congress, Cyber Senate on ICS Security, Nuclear Cyber Security, European Council on Foreign Relations, OpenFest, Last H.O.P.E on water system insecurities and censorship, advises and lectures as an expert for several markets and governments. Chris has been featured in the media with Viceland News' Cyber Warfare series, Hacking the Infrastructure, CNN, Fox News, Asian and European news outlets. The author is currently the Executive Secretary on the board of Geeks Without Bounds and writes for hacking magazines such as 2600 under various pen names.

Printed in the USA
CPSIA information can be obtained
at www.ICGtesting.com
LVHW080833201023
761635LV00012BA/404

9 780995 687547